Help Me Believe

Direct ANSWERS To Real QUESTIONS

Cliffe Knechtle

IVP Books

An imprint of InterVarsity Press
Downers Grove, Illinois

InterVarsity Press
P.O. Box 1400, Downers Grove, IL 60515
World Wide Web: www.ivpress.com
E-mail: email@ivpress.com

InterVarsity Press® is the book-publishing division of InterVarsity Christian Fellowship/USA®, a movement of students and faculty active on campus at hundreds of universities, colleges and schools of nursing in the United States of America, and a member movement of the International Fellowship of Evangelical Students. For information about local and regional activities, write Public Relations Dept., InterVarsity Christian Fellowship/USA, 6400 Schroeder Rd., P.O. Box 7895, Madison, WI 53707-7895, or visit the IVCF website at <www.intervarsity.org>.

All Scripture quotations, unless otherwise indicated, are taken from the Holy Bible, New International Version®. NIV®. *Copyright* ©*1973, 1978, 1984 by International Bible Society. Used by permission of Zondervan Publishing House. All rights reserved.*

ISBN 978-0-8308-2268-3

Printed in the United States of America ∞

Library of Congress Cataloging-in-Publication Data

Knechtle, Cliffe, 1954-
  Help me believe: direct answers to real questions/Cliffe Knechtle.
    p. cm.
  Includes bibliographical references.
  ISBN 0-8308-2268-2 (pbk.: alk. paper)
  1. Apologetics—Miscellanea. 2. Theology—Miscellanea. I. Title.
BT1105.K62 2000
239—dc21   *00-039585*

P	20	19	18	17	16	15	14	13	12	11	10	9	8	7	6	5	4	3
Y	24	23	22	21	20	19	18	17	16	15	14	13	12	11	10	09		

Contents

Preface

People have questions. And there is a lot to ask about in today's world. Life is changing faster than ever, and often we don't know what to make of it. As technology and science map our genetic code and clone people, they raise questions about what it means to be human. As more single-parent homes, same-sex unions and serial relationships develop, we wonder how we can define what a family is.

Everyone seems to have ideas about what's right and what's wrong these days—whether we're talking about abortion or violence or homosexuality. But the biggest sin seems to be intolerance. People can believe whatever they want as long as they don't tell others they are wrong.

Such an atmosphere makes it difficult to talk with people about Christianity. For two millennia the core of Jesus' message has been truth and morality. Today Christians are often characterized as bigots or worse. It's not fashionable to believe that something is true for me and for you.

Despite that, I have become more convinced than ever that people are looking for real meaning in life, solid and lasting relationships, ultimate purpose and truth that you can count on in any situation and for the long haul. There is no security or satisfaction to be found in ideas that change with the weather.

For over twenty years people have been asking me questions about faith—what it means to believe in Jesus. I have tried to answer them honestly. When I don't know the answer, I say so. When I think

Christians have been wrong in the past, I say so. When life is hard and painful, I say so. But I wouldn't be honest if I didn't also give the answers that I am convinced are true about life. That's what this book is about.

I didn't make up the questions in this book. Real people like you asked me about truth, the Bible and God. They asked me about morality, homosexuality and imposing ideas on others. They asked me what makes people so valuable and where the evil came from that we see hurting people all over the world. They asked me why people clash and what can be done about it. They asked me who Jesus is and what he has to do with the problems in the world. They asked me what it means to believe in Jesus, what difference that would make and how I could help them believe.

You'll find their real questions in this book. And you'll find my direct answers, as direct as I know how to be. Maybe you'll find your questions here too, and maybe you'll find clarity as you encounter some of the most important problems any human being can ever face.

Help Me Believe *is dedicated to Ann Walker Knechtle,*
who made this world sweeter
from July 6, 1990, to September 9, 1997.

She is now in the presence of her Lord Jesus.
Heaven is sweeter because Ann is there.

If you play in traffic,

you will end up

on the bumper of a car

regardless of what your mind tells you.

If you do not study

for your exams

but simply allow

the "real, sincere you"

to flow out all over that exam paper,

you will flunk.

1

What is truth?

Truth is relative. You create your own reality. I create my own reality. Don't arrogantly impose your reality on me!"

I often get challenged with words like those as I speak on college and university campuses and talk with students about Christian beliefs. The idea that you and I create our own reality is a popular one, not only on campus but throughout contemporary culture. But does this view work in everyday life?

Suppose you take an exam and allow the "real you" to flow out all over the paper without regard to anything that was taught in the course. The professor might flunk you. If you object, "But I was sincere. This is my view of reality," the professor will respond, "The 'sincere you' was wrong. Your view of reality is incorrect. You flunked."

If a doctor says to you, "We're going to try something brand-new. Take this medicine every day. Come back in two weeks, and we'll see what it has done to you," I think you would begin to feel very nervous.

If as your plane was about to land, the pilot were to announce over the intercom, "We're going to try something different as we land tonight," I think you would get upset very quickly.

You don't want to be a guinea pig for a doctor trying out a new drug. You don't want to be a guinea pig for a pilot trying out a new way of landing a jet. You want both the doctor and the pilot to do that which is reliable, that which has been proven to work. You want both the doctor and the pilot to be in touch with reality.

In order to practice medicine effectively, in order to land a plane safely and in order to pass your exam, you must be in touch with reality. You must not think that you can simply create reality in your own mind. You must be committed instead to using your mind to understand that which is real and true.

The same principle of being in touch with reality holds true for the human quest to know God. God's existence does not depend upon you or me creating God in our minds. God exists separate from our minds.

The Hebrew prophet Jeremiah wrote, "The LORD is the true God; he is the living God, the eternal King" (Jeremiah 10:10). Jeremiah continued, "Every goldsmith is shamed by his idols. His images are a fraud" (v. 14).

A Harvard valedictorian stood before his classmates on graduation day and said, "We've been taught for four years we can believe anything we want as long as we don't believe it's true." If this view is correct—that nothing is correct—then why should I commit myself to anyone or anything? If this view is correct, then all of our dreams and heroes must die, for they are only arbitrary illusions.

But the Bible has a radically different worldview. The Bible insists that reality exists separate from my beliefs. Just because I believe that the world is flat, that does not make it flat. The world is round regardless of what I believe.

Question 1. How can you claim to have the truth?

Some people have insisted that my thinking is too narrow. They tell me, "Cliffe, you are blinded by your Western mindset. You think in 'either-or' categories. Open your mind. Learn to think in 'both-and' categories."

That often leads to sloppy thinking. Two contradictory ideas cannot both be equally true. Either both are wrong, or only one of them is correct. In India pedestrians look both ways before they cross the street. That's because in India, as in the United States, both a bus and a person cannot occupy the same spot at the same time without causing serious bodily damage.

Life does not treat kindly people who believe that reality is only an illusion. If you play in traffic, you will end up on the bumper of a car regardless of what your mind tells you. If you do not study for your exams but simply allow the "real, sincere you" to flow out all over that exam paper, you will flunk regardless of how sincerely you communicate the reality that is in your mind.

You can sit at home refusing to work and insist that you will win the lottery. But unless you get very lucky, you will get very hungry. Life does not treat very kindly those who insist that reality is simply something one creates in one's own mind.

My heroes are those individuals who woke up, smelled the coffee and realized that the greatest reality is the supernatural God. You can read about some of my "reality heroes" in Hebrews 11, which celebrates faithful people of the Old Testament:

By faith Noah, when warned about things not yet seen, in holy fear built an ark to save his family. . . . By faith Abraham, when called to go to a place he would later receive as his inheritance, obeyed and went, even though he did not know where he was going. . . . For he was looking forward to the city with foundations, whose architect and builder is God. By faith Abraham, even though he was past age—and Sarah herself was barren—was enabled to become a father because he considered him faithful who had made the promise. . . . By faith Moses' parents hid him for three months after he was born, because they saw he was no ordinary child, and they were not afraid of the king's edict. By faith Moses, when he had grown up, refused to be known as the son of Pharaoh's daughter. He chose to be mistreated along with the people of God rather than to enjoy the pleasures of sin for a short time. He regarded disgrace for the sake of Christ as of greater value than the treasures of Egypt, because he was looking ahead to his reward. By faith he left

Egypt, not fearing the king's anger; he persevered because he saw him who is invisible. . . . By faith the prostitute Rahab, because she welcomed the spies, was not killed with those who were disobedient.

And a New Testament person, the apostle Paul, wrote toward the end of his life: "For I am already being poured out like a drink offering, and the time has come for my departure. I have fought the good fight, I have finished the race, I have kept the faith. Now there is in store for me the crown of righteousness, which the Lord, the righteous judge, will award to me on that day—and not only to me, but also to all who have longed for his appearing" (2 Timothy 4:6-8).

These people and many others in the Bible lived the most exciting, fulfilling lives possible. Why? Because they lived their lives in light of the reality of God.

We don't create reality in our heads. God has given us minds in order to think clearly, in order to understand what is true and real. Many people search for truth in science, math, medicine and history. But when it comes to God, they give up the search for truth and settle for any fantasy.

In Pittsburgh someone told me, "If you believe the marshmallow man on your right hand gives you happiness and purpose in life, that is great. I would never tell you that what you believe is wrong. It's true for you!" That is a very sad statement. Truth is not created in the mind of the individual.

Jim Jones created an illusion of God that people believed. That illusion was false. It led to the suicidal deaths of over eight hundred people in Guyana. That is a tragedy. That is evil.

David Koresh had an illusion of God in his mind. He created his own god. Too many people believed him. He led his believers to a fiery death in Waco, Texas. That is a tragedy. That is evil.

Because good and evil are so intricately intertwined in this world, you and I must be healthy skeptics. We must not gullibly or blindly believe anyone or anything. We must demand evidence of reliability before we trust.

The evidence is that Jesus Christ is no first-century Jim Jones or

David Koresh. The historical evidence is that Jesus was a consummate gentleman. He treated people with a dignity and a compassion that were outstanding. He brilliantly analyzed the human dilemma as being a problem with perversity rather than simply a problem of perception. His sacrificial death as the only solution for our radical problem with evil demands a response of loyalty and trust.

Because God is real and living, he revealed himself most clearly to us human beings in the form of this man, Jesus of Nazareth. Jesus insisted that when we look at him, we see God. Because God is real and living, he calls us to put our faith in him. The only way to develop a relationship with a living being is to put your faith in that being. If you do not trust a person, you will never get to know the person. God has revealed himself most clearly by becoming a person in Jesus of Nazareth. That is why it is so important that you and I put our faith and trust in Jesus.

Because this point is so important, Jesus repeated it over and over again. Jesus said in John 3:16, "For God so loved the world that he gave his one and only Son, that whoever believes in him shall not perish but have eternal life." Jesus made a remarkable claim: "I am the bread of life. He who comes to me will never go hungry, and he who believes in me will never be thirsty. . . . For my Father's will is that everyone who looks to the Son and believes in him shall have eternal life, and I will raise him up at the last day" (John 6:35, 40). He also said, "I am the light of the world. Whoever follows me will never walk in darkness, but will have the light of life" (John 8:12). Most amazing of all, Jesus claimed this about himself: "I am the resurrection and the life. He who believes in me will live, even though he dies" (John 11:25).

Question 2. Don't all religions teach the same thing?
I am often told that it doesn't matter what religion a person follows because all religions teach the same thing. There are many roads up the mountain, the story goes, but there is only one mountain. There are many beliefs, but they all wind up taking a person to the same place.

Right away we can find some problems with this view. For example, in Islam a man may have four wives. If a man follows Jesus Christ seriously, Jesus allows him to have only one wife. The two religions hold very different views of the marriage bond, the exclusivity of marriage and the status of men and women.

Although there are some similarities among the major world religions, there are clear contradictions. If I say, "All Chinese people look the same," that shows I have not taken the time to get to know Chinese people. In the same way that getting to know people of a particular race or nationality shows us they are not all the same, so a careful reading of the holy books of the major world religions makes it very clear that they contradict each other on some fundamental issues.

In Hinduism and Buddhism the ultimate goal is to become absorbed in the upper ground in an existence called Nirvana. This is a clear denial of the value of the unique individuality of a person because we are all absorbed into the upper ground. But Jesus Christ and authors in the New Testament insist that in heaven you and I will retain our unique individuality. We will have new bodies like the resurrection body of Christ that will live for eternity.

In Hinduism the way to the afterlife is through a cycle of reincarnations, during which time we work off our bad karma. But Jesus Christ revealed that heaven is a free gift that God gives to those who humble themselves and put their faith and trust in Christ.

Muhammad repeatedly stated in the Koran that Jesus is not God but a good prophet. But in the Gospels Jesus by both his words and his actions clearly claims to be God. Either the Koran is correct, or Jesus is correct. They cannot both be correct for they contradict each other.

According to Islam, God would never allow a good prophet like Jesus to die on a cross. But in the Gospels of Matthew, Mark, Luke and John it is crystal clear that Jesus claimed that the key to his life was his death. Jesus insisted that he was born in order to bleed and die on a cross to absorb in his body the just penalty for our sin. In Islam there is no resurrection of Jesus, because Muslims do not believe he died. But one of the central themes of the New Testament is that three days after he died, Jesus physically, bodily rose from the dead.

I want to be open-minded and understand all religious viewpoints. Open-mindedness, however, does not mean that I am so open-minded that my brains fall out. Rather, to be open-minded means that I seriously consider contradictory ideas, examine the evidence and then make my decision based on what the evidence points to as being most reliable.

The bottom-line question is "Who will you and I trust to reveal God accurately?"

Once I was discussing atheism and Christianity in Texas. Someone stepped out of the crowd and announced, "I am an atheist. And Cliffe, you are correct when you say that in atheism life is meaningless, morality is relative and death is the end. You are also correct when you point out that despair and a serious contemplation of suicide are logical consequences of atheism. But I choose to protect myself from those consequences. I choose to play some games. I choose to give my life meaning and to give my life a moral code to live by, and I even choose to view death as not being too horrible. You, Cliffe, play a different game. You create a different illusion. You create God to help make sense of your life."

I responded, "I appreciate your honesty and openness. You have frankly admitted that you are playing games with your life. You cannot face a world where there is no God. So you have grabbed for the 'goodie-goodies' from God in order to make your life more enjoyable. You have openly admitted that you are creating illusions in order to deal with reality. I find your honesty and openness refreshing. Thank you.

"Now I have a wager for you to consider, my game-playing friend. If you are right that there is no God, then when we die, we both go to the same place. We both become dirt. But if I am right, if Jesus Christ revealed God accurately, if Jesus really is the way through death out the other side to eternal life, then when you die, you lose everything, but when I die, I step into the presence of the eternal God. When Jesus Christ returns, you will be judged for your wrongdoing and will spend eternity separate from God. When Jesus Christ returns, I will have to answer to God for the wrong that I have done. I will be equally guilty of doing wrong. But because Jesus bled and died on a cross for my sin, and because I put my faith in him, I will receive eternal life.

"If you are right and Jesus is wrong, you lose nothing, but if you are wrong and Jesus is right, you lose everything. You're a good game player. Put your faith in Christ. You've been dealt a hand of cards in this life. Play the best game you can. It's obvious that the best game in town is being played by those who follow Jesus Christ." This is the line of thinking that Blaise Pascal used.

Someone else in the crowd called out, "That's a lousy reason for believing in Jesus." I responded, "I am not just talking to anybody. I am not talking to every man and every woman. I am talking to a unique individual who has been brutally honest about how he treats life like a big game. If he rejects Christ and atheism is true, he loses nothing. But if he rejects Christ and in reality Jesus is true, then he will lose everything. It is far smarter for my game-playing atheist friend to put his faith in Christ than to hitch his wagon to atheism."

When you read the Gospels and examine how Jesus treated people, how he taught them and the content of his ethical teaching, the way he died on a cross loving and forgiving his enemies, and how he physically rose from the dead, the evidence is very clear that Jesus Christ is a reliable source of information about God in a way that the other options are not. That is why when someone contradicts Jesus, I will follow Jesus every time.

Question 3. Doesn't the Bible mean different things to different people?

A student at the University of Texas in Austin challenged me: "Truth is relative. You create your own reality. You interpret the Bible any way you choose to. I interpret the Bible any way I choose to. You create your own Jesus. I create my own Jesus. It is all relative."

I responded, "I hope that the faculty at the University of Texas teaches you to interpret correctly. I hope they teach you to respect literary style and to read in context. I hope you do not read your biology textbook the same way you read the poetry of Robert Blake. I hope you allow different authors to use different literary styles. I hope you respect their right to communicate differently through different literary styles. I hope that you do not rip one line out of Othello and say, 'This is Shakespeare's worldview.' No.

"You must read in context. You must read the whole work in order to get a proper appreciation of the author's perspective. The same is true as you interpret the Bible. Respect the literary style of poetry used by the psalmist. Respect the right of Jesus to use parable, simile and metaphor. For example, when Jesus says 'Be as wise as serpents and as innocent as doves,' he is not recommending that we slither on our bellies like snakes or that we sprout wings like doves. Instead, Jesus is making a statement about shrewdness and purity."

If I stand on a college campus and call students to commit their lives to Jesus Christ, and then upon finishing my speech I go out and womanize, people have a right to point their fingers at me and say, "Cliffe, you are a hypocrite!" They would be correct. Now suppose I hear their accusations and respond, "It is simply a matter of interpretation. Don't lay your interpretation of Jesus on me." In that case I would simply be playing a game with my accusers. You do not need a Ph.D. in the Gospels to know that Jesus commanded his followers to live sexually pure lives.

Dusko Nikolic, a Croatian policeman otherwise known as "Nasty Nik," said regarding the Serbian residents of his town, "Jesus said, 'Love your neighbors.' Well, I do love them. I love to kill them." You and I do not need to be experts in biblical studies to know that Nikolic is misinterpreting Jesus' command to love our neighbor. He is clearly violating Jesus' moral absolutes.

Truth is not totally relative. You do not create Jesus' teachings in your mind. Jesus spoke very clearly regarding how we are to treat each other. The "interpret Jesus any way you want" game is a dangerous one, for the Bible promises that one day we will stand before God to give an account of the decisions we have made.

Paul said to the Greek philosophers on the Areopagus, "For he [God] has set a day when he will judge the world with justice by the man he has appointed. He has given proof of this to all men by raising him from the dead" (Acts 17:31). God has given us the Ten Commandments, not the Ten Suggestions. We all need Christ's forgiveness, for we have all sinned.

Question 4. How can a loving God judge people?

Some people have the idea that the only people who need God's forgiveness are those infamous people who are headlined on the six o'clock news—financial frauds, war criminals, mass murderers. The idea that we are all going to heaven (except perhaps Hitler, Stalin and Genghis Khan) is a common but mistaken notion.

I have never made the six o'clock news for major crimes or for anything else, but I have done that which is wrong. I am in desperate need of Christ's death on the cross as the payment of the just penalty for my wrongdoing. Whether or not you are famous or infamous, you need Jesus as desperately as I do.

But wait. Isn't God good and loving? If he is, how can he also be wrathful and vengeful toward evil? Is he really going to judge people for their sins?

God's anger over evil is not like a temper tantrum thrown by a spoiled child. God's anger over evil is a result of his inherent goodness and his settled opposition to all evil. Because God is a good God, he must judge evil and destroy it.

In Revelation 20:11-15 we read about the final judgment:

> Then I saw a great white throne and him who was seated on it. Earth and sky fled from his presence, and there was no place for them. And I saw the dead, great and small, standing before the throne and books were opened. Another book was opened, which is the book of life. The dead were judged according to what they had done as recorded in the books. The sea gave up the dead that were in it, and death and Hades gave up the dead that were in them, and each person was judged according to what he had done. Then death and Hades were thrown into the lake of fire. The lake of fire is the second death. If anyone's name was not found written in the book of life, he was thrown into the lake of fire.

Because God's character is good, evil must ultimately be punished and destroyed. Some find it difficult to understand why the penalty for sin is so severe. Because God is totally good, he cannot allow evil to ultimately triumph.

Let's imagine that my wife and I are visitors in your state. While there my wife is horribly murdered. The murderer is caught and tried in a court of law in your home state. The evidence presented clearly points to his guilt. After the jury has pronounced the man guilty, suppose the judge were to stand and say, "It is very clear that you are the murderer. But I free you to leave at once. There will be no penalty for you to pay."

I would be in shock, and so, I hope, would everyone else in the courtroom! The glory of your state would lie in ruins, justice a hollow joke. I would vehemently protest then quickly flee your state for my safety.

I am grateful that the God of the cosmos is deeply committed to the eradication of all evil. God refuses to be intimidated by evil. He will ultimately destroy evil when Jesus returns a second time in power and great glory.

The goodness of God means that evil ultimately loses! The bad news is that I have a problem with evil. The good news is that Jesus Christ died on the cross to absorb the just penalty that I deserve for my wrongdoing.

When a human being begins to understand his or her own problem with perversity and what the death of Jesus on the cross really accomplished, then that person becomes a candidate for heaven.

We all have a real and serious problem with wrongdoing. We deserve death and hell. But Jesus Christ bled and died on the cross to absorb into his body the penalty we deserve, thereby offering us the option of forgiveness. An accurate view of our own wrongdoing and of God's purity produces in us an awareness of our need of Jesus Christ.

Jesus used radical language in describing the cure for the human dilemma. He said that we "must be born again," we must "be saved," we must become "new creatures." The depth of my problems suggests that the radical nature of Christ's cure is necessary.

I have tried to be kind but have run out of kindness. I have tried to forgive but have run out of forgiveness. I have tried to love but have run out of love. I need God; I need Jesus Christ.

Am I capable of selfishness, anger, hatred and violence? Unfortunately I am, and so are all the rest of us. Fortunately there is a good God who wants to make a difference in my life. When we put our faith in Jesus Christ, he helps us become the self-controlled people that God wants us to be. When we put our faith in Jesus Christ, he puts his Holy Spirit in us. It is the Holy Spirit working in partnership with our wills who transforms us into the type of people that down deep we really want to be.

Question 5. Why are you trying so hard to convince me?

I am repeatedly asked, "Cliffe, what motivates you? Why do you go around trying to convince people that Jesus is the way to God?" There are several answers for what compels me—and other Christians—to share Christ with those who don't believe.

A headhunter, a man hired by companies to find needed executives, did his job very well. He would enter the office of a prospective executive and try to get the person relaxed. He would talk about sports, about family. He would lean back in his chair and put his feet up on the table. He would take off his tie. They would have something to drink. They would talk about their favorite vacations. When he had the executive totally relaxed, he would lean across the desk and suddenly ask, "What is the purpose of your life?" The majority of executives would come totally unglued. That was the perfect time to put the vision of the new company before the prospective executive.

One day, the headhunter had an executive totally relaxed. He popped the question, "What is your purpose in life?" Without a moment's hesitation, the executive leaned across the desk, looked the headhunter in the eye and said, "My purpose in life is to go to heaven and to take as many people with me as I can." For the first time in his career the headhunter was tongue-tied!

Jesus Christ came to earth to bring people to heaven; he died on a cross for my sin. I have put my faith in him, and he has given me eternal life in heaven. I am going to heaven, and I want to bring as many people with me as I can. That is a powerful motive for living as I live and doing what I do.

A Christian in Chico, California, brought his best friend to talk with me about how to put one's faith in Christ. The friend asked me some difficult questions. As I patiently tried to answer, suddenly the Christian exclaimed to his friend, "Look, man, I'm going to heaven. It's going to be a blast. I want you to be there with me. I love you, man." The thought of eternal life in heaven is a powerful motive to go there and to bring as many people with you as you possibly can.

Another powerful biblical motive for telling people about the truth in Jesus is what the Bible calls the fear of the Lord. To fear the Lord in a biblical sense means to stand in humility and awe before God. It refers not so much to dread or fright as to profound respect for God.

Insurance companies understand the powerful motive of fear, not in the sense of awe before God but in the sense of anxiety. Anxious fears are a clear sign that I do not stand in proper awe of God. Fear of God produces not anxiety but courage in a person's heart. When you stand in holy awe of God, you do not fear the bump in your body that the doctor says is terminal cancer. When you have a profound understanding of God's power, you do not fear financial loss. When you stand in awe of God's power, you do not fear the loss of a job or the sting of rejection by people.

When we stand in awe of God, fear him and worship him, our lives change. Our behavior begins to reflect the fact that we take God seriously. When you really worship God, your life has to change.

And when you really worship God, you gain a whole new appreciation not only for him but for the people he has created, the people he loves. So when we take God seriously, we begin to take people seriously, and that means we care about people's eternal destiny as well as their fulfillment in this life.

Another biblical motive for telling people about Christ is a sense of duty and responsibility. Because God created us with a free will, we are responsible for the decisions we make. Because God created us with a free will, we will stand before God on the Day of Judgment to give an answer for the way we spent our lives. In Micah 6:8 the prophet wrote,

"And what does the LORD require of you? To act justly and to love mercy and to walk humbly with your God."

Because God has been merciful to each one of us, he requires that we treat each other with mercy. Because God is the Creator and we are the creatures, he requires us to be humble. Our lives are not accidents. God created us for a purpose. When you begin to understand that God created you for a purpose, you begin to grow in your sense of responsibility to live out God's purpose.

Another biblical motive for sharing Christ is simply love. Jesus said in John 14:15, "If you love me, you will obey what I command." The Bible has an uncanny way of linking spirituality with morality. My love for God will be on display in the way I love people.

Love for Jesus is a powerful motive to love people. The apostle John wrote, "This is how we know what love is: Jesus Christ laid down his life for us. And we ought to lay down our lives for our brothers. . . . Dear children, let us not love with words or tongue but with actions and in truth" (1 John 3:16, 18).

God loves. Because God created us in his image, he wired us in such a way that love should be one of our most powerful motives in life.

It is too easy to stop loving, to stop caring, to stop serving. Isn't it amazing to consider the God whom Jesus revealed? He loves you and me with an unconditional love, with an eternal love, with a love that does not grow hot or cold depending on his mood swings, with a love that is patient, with a love that forgives and with a love that never, never quits. This is an absurd love. It is almost too good to be true because human love is so fickle. But it is the quality of love that every one of us longs for.

It was love that motivated the Father to send his only Son Jesus to earth to rescue you and me. It was love that motivated Jesus Christ to bleed and die on the cross to give you and me eternal life. Jesus loves you; Jesus loves me. Motivated by love, you and I can put our trust in him. Motivated by love, you and I can obey Jesus. Love for Jesus and for people is a powerful motive for a follower of Christ.

My experience shows me
that people refer to values and
morals outside of themselves.
People frequently
use the words *should* and *ought;*
these words clearly point
to values outside
both the individual and a given society,
for frequently
should and *ought* are applied
in a judgment
of our own society.

2

How can you tell me
what's right & wrong?

Thomas Jefferson had some appreciation for the Bible. But he cut out of the Bible all references to the holiness of God, the sinfulness of man and the need for Christ's forgiveness through his death on the cross. Jefferson viewed these concepts as primitive and unnecessary for rational human beings.

Jefferson's denial of sin worked its way into the fabric of his life. His dear sister Lucy married Dr. Charles Lewis, a physician and planter. The couple moved to Kentucky with their two sons, Lilburn and Aishem, where they worked on a plantation. Suddenly Lucy died, and Charles moved back to the East Coast leaving his two sons to run the plantation.

One day George, a slave, accidentally dropped one of Lucy's favorite pitchers. Lilburn and Aishem decided to teach all their slaves a lesson about the consequences of such a mistake. They took George to the meat house and butchered him before the watching eyes of the other slaves.

Thomas Jefferson was unable to deal with the butchering of that slave by his two nephews. He had such an optimistic view of human nature that he could not comprehend what they had done. Despite his other great personal qualities and gifts, Jefferson deceived himself regarding his own sinful nature and the sinful nature of his two nephews. God calls us to have a different view of evil than Jefferson had. He calls us not to deny evil but to hate it.

Does that mean that Christians hate sinners? Of course not—or at least we shouldn't. I hate the evil in me, but I affirm my value as a human being created in the image of God and loved by God. I hate the evil in you, but I affirm your value as a human being created in the image of God and loved by Jesus. I hate the evil that Pol Pot committed in Cambodia; I affirm the value of a human being named Pol Pot created in the image of God. I detest the atrocities that Adolf Hitler carried out; I affirm the worth of the person named Adolf Hitler created in God's image. I abhor the wicked acts that Joseph Stalin performed; I affirm the value of the man named Joseph Stalin whom God created in his image.

I hate cancer because cancer is destructive. Why do I hate evil? Because evil is destructive. To be tolerant of people does not mean to embrace the evil they do. To be tolerant means to respect people's right to choose to believe whatever they want to believe. But Jesus calls you and me to hate evil. God takes evil seriously. God must judge evil because God is good. I do not know why God chose to use the Israelites to judge the Canaanites, Philistines, Hittites, Amorites and others at that time in that way. But I do know that because God is good, he must punish evil.

I am so grateful that Jesus Christ bled and died on a cross to pay the penalty I deserve for my evil. I have put my faith in Christ and accepted his forgiveness. I have accepted Christ's payment for my wrongdoing when he bled and died on the cross. My prayer is that you have made the same decision.

Question 6. What gives you the right to impose your morality on others?

People often get impatient with me when I talk about morality. They ask, "How can you tell somebody else what's right and wrong? What gives you the right to impose your values on another person?"

We live in a culture deeply committed to moral relativism. But even in this highly morally relativistic culture there are at least two closely related moral absolutes. One of those moral absolutes is "You must be tolerant of all behavior." The other moral absolute is "Thou shalt not judge."

Yet most human beings insist that there must be at least a few additional moral absolutes. The only way there can be any moral absolute is if there is some type of God or gods to create and define these intangible values we call moral absolutes. In order to have morality you have to first have an intelligent mind to define what is right and what is wrong. If there was no conscious mind prior to the human mind, then it is the human mind that creates and defines morality. This means that morality is relative.

If morality is totally relative, then "right" and "wrong" become the simple biases and prejudices of the individual. But when a person acknowledges that God has created the values of justice, goodness and kindness, then the challenge is for the individual to use his or her conscience, common sense and reason to understand what is right in a given situation.

When a person has an accurate view of God's character and a desire to grow in faith, that person's life will be marked by a desire to "cling to what is good" (Romans 12:9). Quite often when people think that their mind is becoming more open, it is simply a case of their conscience corroding. Paul wrote, "To the pure, all things are pure, but to those who are corrupted and do not believe, nothing is pure. In fact, both their minds and consciences are corrupted" (Titus 1:15). A growing faith in Jesus Christ will be marked by a conscience that is becoming more sensitive to the great gulf between good and evil.

Woody Allen's movie *Crimes and Misdemeanors* gives a frightening picture of the killing of a conscience. Judah Rosenthal is a successful ophthalmologist with a lovely wife, a beautiful family and all the perks that come from a successful medical practice. But he also has a mistress on the side. One day she threatens to expose their relationship to Judah's wife. In his panic Judah turns to his rabbi for counsel. The rabbi encourages him to confess his sin to God and to his wife, pointing out that God and his wife can forgive. Judah is unwilling to take the risk of revealing his affair. Further, he is not looking for forgiveness; he is looking for an escape. He remembers as a child listening to the rabbi teach, "God is always watching you." But Judah is more afraid of disturbing his smooth lifestyle than of standing before a wrathful God.

Judah presents his dilemma to his brother, who is in organized crime. The brother offers to have the mistress killed. Judah agonizes. But as she increases the pressure, he finally gives in; she must be silenced. A hit man does the dirty deed. Judah goes to the apartment of the murdered mistress to gather any evidence of their affair. Seeing her lying on the floor with her eyes open in the blank stare of death, he begins to comprehend that he has done a terrible thing. He begins to realize that there is very little difference between Nazis who gassed Jews in Auschwitz and himself.

The pressure in his conscience begins to build. If he does not confess his sin, he will have a nervous breakdown. But he wiggles out of both of those horrible options by killing his conscience. At the end of the movie, the Rosenthal family is seated around the table. Judah and his wife and children are smiling, laughing, and having a great time. The only problem is, Judah has killed his conscience.

Crimes and Misdemeanors is the account of a double murder: the murder of a woman and the murder of a man's conscience. Judah's life unfolds in three neat steps. First, deny God. Kill God—not in an act of violence, but simply by acting as if God does not exist. If God does not exist, then there is no mind prior to the human mind to define what is right and wrong. It therefore follows that it is the human mind that creates the categories of right and wrong.

This leads to the second step: Judah defines right and wrong according to his own desires. There is no absolute value of justice or compassion. Justice and compassion are created and defined by the individual. Judah defines right and wrong according to his needs. He is a pragmatist. Therefore, justice must be defined in such a way that his lifestyle can be maintained. Self-interest is the criteria he uses to define right and wrong, justice and compassion.

The third step is awkward but easily accomplished. Kill your conscience. That is the only way to get rid of the awkward feelings of guilt. To carry off his plan smoothly Judah Rosenthal denies God's existence, rationalizes that evil can actually be good and kills his conscience. It worked to have the mistress murdered; therefore, it was good. After Judah dispenses with God and moral absolutes, all he has to do is get rid of his conscience. Curing pangs of guilt was a short and efficient process.

You and I live in a culture that has tried to get rid of God, has defined right and wrong in terms of what will bring the quickest personal gain, and has discarded such notions as sin and guilt. No wonder America cannot tell right from wrong. Jesus insisted that human beings have value because God created them in his image. Jesus also insisted that justice and integrity are real values that God has created.

Good values flow from the good character of God. Jesus wants to make us spiritually alive to himself. He claimed to be God reaching out to people who have tried to get rid of God but who have found that life falls apart without God. Jesus comes to people who have enough conscience to be aware of the fact that they have at times done wrong. He does not come to condemn; he comes to forgive. He comes to free us from evil and to free us to live a life of doing what is right.

Question 7. Why do Christians get so upset about homosexuality?

First of all, the value of a human being has nothing to do with his or her sexual practice. Instead, the value of a human being is based on the fact that we all are created in the image of God. Our value comes from the fact that God created us for a purpose, which is loving and worshiping him, and loving and serving each other.

In the same way that God created our lives for a purpose, he also created our sexuality for a purpose. In Genesis 2:24, concerning the creation of Adam and Eve, we read that "For this reason a man will leave his father and mother and be united to his wife, and they will become one flesh."

God created us male and female in order that we might make a life-long commitment to each other. Within that lifelong commitment we are to enjoy sexuality as a gift from God. The practice of homosexual sex is a perversion of the gift of human sexuality that God has given us.

In fact, heterosexual lust is also a perversion of this God-given gift. Many people have twisted the gift of sexuality. Homosexuals have twisted that gift through their practice of homosexuality. I, as a hetero-sexual male, have perverted and twisted that gift through my hetero-sexual lust. But the great news of the New Testament is that Jesus Christ bled and died on a cross to forgive both my homosexual friend and me.

While I was at a speaking engagement in Arizona, two lesbians seated in front of me said, "We were born lesbians. Certainly you cannot tell us that this is wrong." I asked them, "Are you telling me that simply because we have a natural drive, that makes it right?" They said, "If we are born with a natural drive, that means God created us that way. Therefore, that natural drive is good and right."

I asked them, "Do you think that my natural heterosexual drive motivates me to have sex with just one woman all my life?" They got the point. I don't know any heterosexual men or women whose sex drive motivates them to have sex with just one person. Just because a drive comes naturally to us does not make it right.

When I was six years old, I did something that I had never seen modeled for me. I picked up a package of gum, slipped it into my pocket and walked out of the store. Stealing came very naturally to me. That does not make it right. We are all born with what Dallas Willard, professor of philosophy at the University of Southern California, called "a readiness to sin factor."

The thoughtful person must ask, "What is the purpose for which God made me? What is the purpose of the sexuality that God gave me? What is the purpose of the tongue that God has given me? What is the purpose of the emotions God has given me?" If losing my temper comes naturally to me, that does not mean that losing my temper is good. The question becomes "What is the purpose for which God gave me the different gifts that I have?"

Someone once handed me a book entitled *All That Jesus Said About Homosexuality*. When I opened the book, I discovered that all the pages were blank.

Although Jesus never mentioned the word *homosexual* in the Gospels, he used a broad term for sexual immorality when he said, "For from within, out of men's hearts, come evil thoughts, sexual immorality . . ." (Mark 7:21). The Greek word for "sexual immorality" is *porneia*. It encompasses all forms of sexual immorality.

It is abundantly clear that Jesus viewed the Old Testament, the Torah, as the Word of God. He consistently quoted the Old Testament as the Word of God. And because he was a teacher of the Torah (the Jewish law), Jesus could not possibly have approved of homosexual practice. The Torah commands, "Do not lie with a man as one lies with a woman; that is detestable" (Leviticus 18:22) and "If a man lies with a man as one lies with a woman, both of them have done what is detestable" (Leviticus 20:13). The word *detestable* conveys a clear moral judgment regarding the sin of homosexual practice. This is not a culturally relative position. Instead, it is a moral imperative that is binding across all cultures throughout all time.

The Jews' insistence upon monogamous heterosexual marriages made them distinct from the ancient cultures that surrounded them. The ancient Greeks and Romans viewed sex not as an interaction between a man and a woman but rather as something one did to someone else. They were not concerned about the gender of the sex partner; rather they were concerned about the distinction between active and passive roles in sex. That is why boys and women were very often treated interchangeably as the objects of male desire. Julius Caesar was known as every woman's man and every man's man. Plato wrote about Socrates' delight in having sex with little boys. By contrast, the Jews believed in following God's command to enjoy sex only within a heterosexual monogamous lifelong relationship.

God's judgment on homosexual practice continues consistently in the New Testament. The apostle Paul wrote about people who had given themselves over to sin: "God gave them over to shameful lusts. Even their women exchanged natural relations for unnatural ones. In the same way the men also abandoned natural relations with women and were inflamed with lust for one another. Men committed indecent acts with other men, and received in themselves the due penalty for their perversion" (Romans 1:26-27).

By contrast, in the book of Genesis we have a beautiful statement regarding the purpose for human sexuality:

> So the LORD God caused the man to fall into a deep sleep; and while he was sleeping, he took one of the man's ribs and closed up the place with flesh. Then the LORD God made a woman from the rib he had taken out of the man, and he brought her to the man.
> The man said,
>
> "This is now bone of my bones
>   and flesh of my flesh;
> she shall be called 'woman,'
>   for she was taken out of man."
>
> For this reason a man will leave his father and mother and be united to his wife, and they will become one flesh. (Genesis 2:21-24)

In this very simple but profound passage God defines marriage as a heterosexual monogamous relationship that is to last until death. A man is to acknowledge his commitment to the woman as he leaves his father and mother, and he is to permanently seal that commitment as he is united with his wife. They will physically consummate their marriage by becoming one flesh. The Bible gives us no other pattern for marriage or sexual intercourse. God has provided no alternative.

Still some people insist, "Sexual repression is unhealthy." But the apostle Paul wrote about the value of bringing our bodily drives under control:

> Do you not know that in a race all the runners run, but only one gets the prize? Run in such a way as to get the prize. Everyone who competes in

the games goes into strict training. They do it to get a crown that will not last; but we do it to get a crown that will last forever. Therefore, I do not run like a man running aimlessly; I do not fight like a man beating the air. No, I beat my body and make it my slave so that after I have preached to others, I myself will not be disqualified for the prize. (1 Corinthians 9:24-27)

Paul was saying that if we are striving for a worthy goal, then the sacrifice is a delight. Self-control and self-limitation are the only basis for an athlete's hope of winning.

Self-control is not repressive or psychologically hazardous when a person is aiming for a valuable prize. When the goal is sufficiently worthy, self-control is not an evil; it is part of the realistic process of achieving that goal. When we realize that the all-wise God is good and loves us, then we understand that it is beneficial to exercise self-control in the use of our sexuality. God has our best interests in mind when he limits sexual intercourse to a monogamous, heterosexual lifelong relationship.

In order to trust God with our sexuality we must answer the questions, "Is the God whom Jesus revealed really good? Does he really love us? Does he really have our best interests in mind?" The obvious answers that Jesus revealed are "Yes. God does love you. Yes, God is good. Yes, God does have your best interests in mind." Therefore, obeying Jesus is the path to the happiest, the most fulfilling, the most exciting life possible.

Question 8. Where do moral values come from?

Values are convictions that deeply affect behavior. Where do those values come from? Do values come from inside the individual or from outside? If they come purely from within—if there is no God who determines what is right and wrong—then values are relative.

If values come from within each individual, there are several places they can come from. First, they can come from biological drives.

In North Carolina I asked a crowd, "What motivated Mother Teresa to work among the dying on the streets of Calcutta, India?" Someone replied, "Mother Teresa was motivated by a drive to preserve the genetic pool." I heard some stifled laughter.

Adolf Hitler justified his enormous cruelty by asking, "Why should I not be more cruel than nature itself?" He saw that nature is cruel and succeeded at going beyond even what seemed natural. We have the ability, like Mother Teresa, to break away from what seems to be purely natural instinct and to execute unique deeds as individuals. While we abhor the behavior of Hitler, we stand in awe of the behavior of Mother Teresa.

The philosopher Immanuel Kant also held that values come from inside the individual; however, he believed they come from a person's reasoning. In other words, moral values are based on human reason. Let's examine that position.

When Hurricane Andrew swept through Florida, some of the houses in its path remained intact. However, other houses lost their roofs. Close investigation revealed that many of the houses that lost their roofs had been put together by builders who did not follow the building code and did not use the necessary hardware. They never thought they would be caught, but Hurricane Andrew exposed the shortcuts they had taken. Their reasoning was simple: "If we leave out some of the hardware, the houses will still stand, and we will make more profit."

In his perceptive book *Why Johnny Can't Tell Right from Wrong* ([New York: Simon & Schuster, 1992], pp. 14, 25), William Kilpatrick writes, "Twenty-one percent of all secondary school students avoid using the restrooms out of fear of being harmed or intimidated. Surveys of school children reveal that their chief school-related concern is the disruptive behavior of their classmates. Teachers have similar concerns. Almost one-third of public school teachers indicate that they have seriously considered leaving teaching because of student misbehavior." We have succumbed to a myth that claims that morality comes naturally, or at most, with the help of a little reasoning. But it seems increasingly clear that these metaphors and the models that flow from them aren't working. As William Kilpatrick wrote, "The 'natural' thing to do in most situations is to take the easy way out. The most perfectly rational plan of action is to always put yourself first."

The French philosopher Jean-Jacques Rousseau also believed that values come from within the individual. But instead of turning to reason or nature for the source, Rousseau turned to human feelings. He maintained that children are born with pure feelings that form the basis of real values. They are born naturally good. But the more Rousseau interacted with children, the more difficult he found it to tolerate their selfish behavior. In fact, he reached the point where he chose to abandon all five of his own children. Paul Johnson, in his work *Intellectuals* ([New York: Harper & Row, 1998], pp. 21, 22), writes:

> The shelter that received Rousseau's five children was overwhelmed by abandoned infants, over three thousand a year. In 1758 Rousseau himself noted that the total had risen to 5,082. By 1772 it averaged nearly 8,000. Two-thirds of the babies died in their first year. An average of fourteen out of every hundred survived to the age of seven, and of these five grew to maturity, most of them becoming beggars and vagabonds. Rousseau did not even note the dates of the births of his five children and never took any interest in what happened to them, except once in 1761, when he believed Therese (their mother) was dying and made a perfunctory attempt, soon discontinued, to use a note to discover the whereabouts of the first child.

Although Rousseau believed that children are born pure, his experience with children contradicted his belief. The Bible teaches that we all have a Jekyll and Hyde personality. Because we are created in the image of God, we all at times have the capacity to do that which is good. Because we are also born with a sinful nature, we all at times choose to do evil. Our feelings get confused. At times we feel that evil is good and that good is really evil. Feelings alone are not an adequate basis for morality.

More recently some youths in New York City did not have enough money to get into a dance hall. They walked to a subway station and pulled knives on a family visiting the city. After robbing them and murdering one member of the family, the youths used the stolen money to enter the dance hall. Police arrested them while they were dancing. If feelings are really the basis of values and morals, whose feelings are we going to trust? Does a strong desire to go dancing justify stealing and murder in order to get the money to be admitted to the dance hall?

The German philosopher Friedrich Nietzsche argued that values come from the exercise of the individual's will. He saw the raw power of our ability to decide as being the basis for values and morals. This view too has serious shortcomings.

A truck driver saw a woman in distress on the side of the road. After stopping to give her some "roadside assistance," he exercised his will by raping her and then murdering her.

Do values really come from inside the individual, from our drive to preserve our genes, from our ability to reason, or to feel, or to exercise a powerful will? If that is true, then all values and morals are relative.

Repeatedly, however, my experience shows me that people refer to values and morals outside of themselves. People frequently use the words *should* and *ought*; these words clearly point to values outside both the individual and a given society, for frequently *should* and *ought* are applied in a judgment of our own society.

Jesus and the Bible insist that values and morals come from outside the individual. They flow from the character of our good and loving God. Because God is love, when he created us, he gave us the innate ability to genuinely love. According to Jesus Christ, love is not open to being redefined by builders in Florida, by a French philosopher who abandons his children, by youths in New York City who want to go to a dance or by a truck driver who decides to rape and murder. God has chosen to define for us clearly what real love is.

When Jesus was bleeding and dying on a cross, two thieves were hung on either side of him. The first turned to him and said, "If you really are the Son of God, get us and yourself off these crosses." The second criminal turned to first criminal and said, "You fool. We bleed and die here because we deserve it. But this Jesus is the innocent, holy, pure Son of God." Then the second criminal turned to Jesus and pleaded, "Remember me when you come into your kingdom." Jesus responded, "I tell you the truth. Today you will be with me in Paradise."

When the second criminal turned to Jesus expressing his need for forgiveness, Jesus' value system was on the line. He could have easily looked the man in the face and said, "Forget it, you scumball. You have committed grotesque evil. You die because you deserve it." But Jesus valued that criminal. He valued him so highly that he was bleeding and dying on the cross to forgive him. That is why Jesus responded to the criminal, "I tell you the truth. Today you will be with me in Paradise."

Jesus values you and me so highly that he bled and died on a cross to pay the price to buy us back from sin and hell. Now the responsibility is on our shoulders. We must make a decision of the will to ask Christ for forgiveness, to put our faith in him and to commit our lives to follow him as the truth.

That is the decision Jesus calls you and me to make. That is the way to begin a spiritual relationship with the living God. That is the way to receive eternal life. That is the way to allow God to resurrect your conscience and to sensitize it. That is the way to open up your life so that the power of God might enable you to do that which is right instead of giving in to that which is wrong.

Why is life important?

Because it is

a gift from the God who loves you.

Why is life important?

Because God

has given all human life dignity.

Therefore,

we must treat each other justly.

Why is life important?

Because the God

at the heart of the universe

loves us.

Therefore, he created us

to love him and to love each other.

3

Why is life so valuable?

P*resident Clinton conducted an MTV press conference. At first the young* people asked him rather humorous questions. They asked him about his underwear and his favorite rock songs.

The mood of the press conference changed, however, when seventeen-year-old Dalia Schweitzer asked, "Mr. President, it seems to me that Kurt Cobain's recent suicide exemplified the emptiness that many in our generation feel. How do you propose to teach our youth how important life is?"

President Clinton almost gagged on his tongue. The question was a profound one addressing the significance of human existence. Fortunately, the president did not try to propose a legislative answer to the question. Instead, he turned to some positive think therapy, calling young people to a feeling that they are the most important person in the world to somebody else.

The problem with that view is that the significance of human life, the purpose of human existence, cannot be reduced to a matter of feeling good about ourselves.

A phenomenally popular rock star, Kurt Cobain had every reason to feel good about himself. Millions of fans thought he was the greatest musician alive. He frequently used alcohol and other drugs to make himself feel good. But obviously good feelings were not enough to give Kurt Cobain a reason to keep on living.

Dalia Schweitzer's question was more than a casual inquiry about President Clinton's personal opinions; it was clearly a direct attack at the underbelly of secularism. Secularism insists that happiness is found in making money and buying expensive toys. Our secular culture would condemn us to looking for happiness only in this world.

Jesus warned repeatedly that we are easily consumed by material things. When we lean on clothing and food to try to fill a starving spirit, we will shrivel spiritually. A full belly does not fill a starving spirit. That is why Jesus called us not to focus our lives on food and clothing but rather to seek first God's rule in our lives. Christ calls us to come alive spiritually to God by putting our faith in him and by surrendering to his rule in our lives.

Question 9. What difference does it make if life is valuable or not?

God gave us bodies and put us in a position of responsibility to care for them. Our bodies are good gifts from God to be treated appropriately. But there is so much more to human existence than simply the physical.

We have rational minds, wills, emotions, consciences and souls. And Jesus asked the penetrating question, "What does it profit a man or a woman if they gain the whole world, but lose their soul?" The fact is that God created you and me for a purpose: to love and worship God, and to love and serve each other.

The Hebrew prophet Micah wrote, "What does the LORD require of you? To act justly and to love mercy and to walk humbly with your God" (Micah 6:8). God created us to act toward each other with justice. Justice is respecting the dignity of human life.

The only reason that human life has dignity is because it has been created by God for a reason, for a purpose. Life is not an accident; it is a gift from God. Therefore, handle life with the greatest of care. On the Day of Judgment, God will hold us responsible for whether or not we treated our lives and the lives of others with dignity.

As America moves away from God, it moves away from an understanding of the dignity of life. We are becoming a brutal nation. Gun violence is a growing American problem. Talk show host Johnny Carson put it this way: "You can get more with a kind word and a gun than you can with a kind word alone." Obviously a lot of people in our country agree with Johnny Carson. Every seventh person you pass on the street in America is carrying a weapon either on their person or in their car.

Americans not only carry weapons, they use their weapons. In 1990 handguns killed only 22 people in Great Britain, 68 in Canada and 87 in Japan. However, in 1990 handguns killed 10,567 people in the United States! In 1998 and 1999 there was an epidemic of school and workplace mass shootings. A society's understanding of the dignity of human life either encourages or discourages violent behavior. In the United States there's a cowboy mentality that says, "Get out of my way or I'll blow you away."

However, to act justly means that I refuse to devalue people by blowing them away if they don't move out of my way. Their lives are more important than my desire to have them out of my way.

Because awe of God is disappearing, brutal behavior is increasing. Donald Jensen enjoyed umpiring Little League baseball. Unfortunately, one day he was struck in the head by a bat that was deliberately thrown by one of the young players. Later that night he was hospitalized.

While in the hospital that night for observation, Donald Jensen wrote a thoughtful letter. Part of the letter reads, "The purpose of Little League is to teach baseball skills to young men. Obviously, a team which does not play well in a given game, and is given the opportunity to blame that loss on an umpire for one call or two, is being given the chance to take all responsibility for the loss from their shoulders. A parent or adult leader who permits the young player to blame his failures on an umpire . . . is doing the worst kind of injustice to that youngster. . . . This irresponsibility is bound to carry over to future years."

That is pure wisdom coming from a Little League umpire. The next time you are tempted to berate an umpire, remember him—the late Donald Jensen. The next morning he died of a brain concussion.

In the United States we have an entertainment industry that plays upon the human lust for violence. We have a sin problem, and the entertainment industry understands how to make money by feeding off that sin problem.

Extreme violence has become commonplace in films and on television. In a disturbing trend, movies and TV programs frequently encourage sadistic laughter among viewers—at cruel behavior, extreme physical pain and even the horrible murder of human beings. This is so familiar that I will mention only one example. In the movie *Another 48 Hours* Eddie Murphy stops a fight in a bar by shooting one of the troublemakers in the leg. As the man collapses on the floor shrieking and writhing in pain, Eddie Murphy glibly says, "Sorry about the kneecap. I got a little excited." The audience is expected to laugh sarcastically, but that sarcastic laughter over the pain of a human being only reveals our view of the cheapness of human life.

Violence in America is also promoted by a runaway individualism. John Donne wrote in 1624, "No man is an island, entire of itself; every man [or woman] is a piece of the continent, a part of the main. . . . Any man's [or woman's] death diminishes me, because I am involved in mankind; and therefore never send to know for whom the bell tolls; it tolls for thee."

In American culture many people have the attitude they are islands, that each person is totally self-sufficient. To express a need for others is a sign of weakness; to be totally independent is admired. To be involved in other people's lives is smart—if those other people can help you get ahead; to be involved in the lives of people who cannot help you get ahead is a waste of your time. This runaway individualism leads to isolation, to a refusal to be involved in significant ways in other people's lives.

Why is life important? Because it is a gift from the God who loves you. Why is life important? Because God has given all human life dignity. Therefore, we must treat each other justly. Why is life important? Because the God at the heart of the universe loves us. Therefore, he created us to love him and to love each other.

Todd Pheipers wrote in the *Denver Post*:

> Almost always, the answer was the same. "How did your game go?" I'd ask. "Good," he would reply. "How did you do?" . . . "Good." The response wasn't a curt put-off, nor was it a rote reaction. It was offered honestly and almost always with enthusiasm. . . . It didn't matter if the final score was 1-0 or 100-1. It didn't matter if he had knocked home the winning run or if he had struck out every time at bat. It didn't matter if the subject was sports, or school, or family or something else. "How were things?" . . . "Good." He had so much perspective for a little boy . . . sports were like the rest of life. Taking part was what made it worthwhile. . . . Gus found happiness just in taking part. It wasn't just sports. It was choir and student council at school. It was violin lessons. It was a birthday party at a friend's house. . . . Every day was a new day, a time for a new experience. Life was good. But life ended for a positive and uncomplaining and involved little boy last Sunday in a fire in Silver Plume, Colorado. There were so many things undone. . . .We hadn't made our trek north to watch the dirt races at Erie, Colorado. . . . What we had done, though, was communicate through ten short years. And we had ended every night we were together with the same words: "I love you." Please let me say it one more time. Gus, I love you.

Why is life important? Because God created us to walk humbly with him for eternity, enjoying him and each other.

Question 10. What do you think about abortion?
The question comes up persistently: "What do you think about abortion? Is it right or wrong?"

If abortion is simply removing excess skin, then the answer is simple: obviously there is nothing wrong with abortion. I remove excess skin from my body regularly. I peel my calluses. I cut my toenails and fingernails. However, if abortion is ending a human life because of the motivations of convenience or selfishness, then I am convinced we can all agree that abortion is wrong.

So the first question we have to ask is, "When does human life begin?" According to the simplest definition of human life agreed upon in almost every major medical center around the world, if a body lying on a bed in an intensive care unit has both brain activity and heartbeat, doctors and nurses are legally, ethically and morally responsible to do everything within their power to sustain that life. Brain activity and a heartbeat are clear indications of human life.

Between four and six weeks after conception, the "little piece of skin" in a woman's womb begins to display both brain activity and a heartbeat. According to the simplest definition of human life, that is already a human being.

But what about the period before four to six weeks? At that point is it simply a piece of skin, or is it a human life? What is the difference between a one-minute-old fertilized egg, a four-week-old fertilized egg and you? The only difference is in degree of maturation. You were at a different but proper stage of development at one minute, at four weeks, at nine months and at twenty years, but you were still a human being, not something else. One hundred times out of one hundred, if that fertilized egg stays healthy, it eventually passes down the woman's birth canal as a human being, never as an alligator or as a puppy dog. Regardless of whether you are one minute old, four months old or four years old, you are at a particular stage of development for a human life.

When we address the issue of abortion, the fundamental question is, "Do we really have a human life in the woman's womb?" I am convinced the overwhelming evidence points to that life in a woman's womb as being a human life.

Someone in Minnesota objected to my viewpoint by claiming, "Human life is that life which can sustain itself, which can live on its own." I responded, "My one-year-old baby boy cannot live on his own. He is dependent upon his mother and father to feed, clean and care for him. Does that mean that he is not a real person?"

Fortunately, our society has strict laws that protect my son from abuse and neglect, but before he passed down his mother's birth canal, he was growing in the most dangerous place on the planet. The laws of our land protect a person's right to poison, burn to death and hack to pieces an unborn baby on the other side of the birth canal. So my advice to all you thumb-sucking, gymnastically inclined unborn babies is, "Stop sucking your thumb and doing somersaults in your mother's womb! Get to the other end of the birth canal so that you will be protected by law from being poisoned, burned or hacked to death. Hurry!"

With an agitated tone in her voice a woman in North Carolina said, "Look at the plight of those urban babies born into single-parent families or into no family at all! You must allow abortion to happen among the urban poor!"

I responded, "I am all too aware of the very difficult start in life that many children have when they are born into this world. When God instituted the family, he did not have in mind one parent or no parents. He clearly designed the family to have a father and a mother loving each other and loving their children. In many situations we are confronted by some gigantic problems. Immediately following the Civil War there was a gigantic problem of unemployment among the freed slaves. The solution for the very high rate of unemployment among African Americans was not to enslave them again. We had to creatively work hard to find better solutions."

A child born into a home where Mom and Dad hate each other, where there is only one struggling single parent or where there are no parents at all has the odds stacked against him or her. But the solution to this horrible problem is not to murder the child. There have to be better, more creative solutions. All the good solutions will involve personal sacrifice. God created us to love and sacrifice for each other. We must be ready to financially sacrifice for children who have been given a most difficult start in life.

At the University of Pennsylvania a woman professor interrupted me with a loud voice: "You are a fundamentalist Christian. You are a white male. You have no right to stand on this campus and communicate that abortion is wrong." I stood silently for about ten seconds trying to gather my thoughts.

Suddenly, from behind me, the voice of a woman rang clear: "I am not a fundamentalist Christian. I am not a white male. I am strongly opposed to abortion. I resent your implication that the only people who are opposed to abortion are fundamentalist Christians and white males. Abortion is clearly the murder of a human life. I am opposed to all murder." The professor stood there in silence. She had tried to use emotional demagoguery on me, but another woman had spoken up and countered what was basically an emotional attack.

In the same breath that I speak against abortion, I must speak for adoption. Adoption is a wonderful alternative to abortion: it promotes life instead of dealing out death.

We should encourage all people to be prochoice: before you have sex, you make a choice. Before you have sex, you make a lifelong commitment to that person. That was God's plan when he created us male and female.

Any dog can have sex with a lot of dogs. It takes a human being, created in the image of God, to make an intentional lifelong commitment to one spouse. That is God's design in creating us male and female. To divorce sex from a lifelong commitment is to dehumanize both yourself and your sex partner. Jesus Christ calls us to exercise our power of choice in a very responsible way. He is wise. You can trust him: he wants to give you the best life possible.

In Georgia someone once asked me, "How do you think through the issue of abortion if the mother's life is in danger?"

I have a friend who, along with his wife, was excited about the birth of their first child. The delivery was going smoothly, so smoothly that he left the delivery room to get a drink. When he returned moments later, the situation had changed dramatically. The doctor looked at him and asked one of the most difficult questions imaginable: "Whose life do you want me to save? Your wife's or your child's?" My friend responded quickly, "Doctor, save my wife first. Then try to save our child." Tragically, the doctor was unable to save either life; both the mother and the baby died. However, I strongly support my friend's decision to ask the doctor to first save the life of his wife. She had put herself in a position to bring the child into the world; she had sacrificed to bear that child. Also, my first commitment is to my wife. For these reasons I completely support his decision.

Some make the argument "The unborn baby is part of the mother's body. The mother has the right to do with her body as she chooses." Yes the mother does have the right to do with her own body as she chooses. But is the unborn baby really part of the mother? After thirty days the body of the baby has its own circulatory system. The waste flows into the mother; nutrients flow into the baby. The mother does not give the baby her blood; the baby has his or her own blood. If the baby is really part of the mother's body, then the mother while pregnant has four eyes, four ears, two noses and four legs. And if the baby is a boy, then the mother has a penis. The unborn baby is obviously not simply part of the mother.

Do you support a person's right to find out the sex of a child and then to abort the child if it is female? How do you feel about the government of a state in India legislating that no doctor is allowed to perform amniocentesis to determine the sex of an unborn child? In that part of India, when many families found out that their unborn child was female, they would abort. The government stepped in and said, "No longer." I am very grateful for that law helping to prevent the abortion of female fetuses. I am convinced that all human life—be it male or female—has equal value and dignity, because all human life is created in the image of God.

In Madison, Wisconsin, someone asked me, "What about rape? Are you going to tell a woman that she has to bear a child that is the result of her being raped?"

It is very rare for conception to take place after a rape, but it does occur occasionally. A fourteen-year-old girl was raped, became pregnant and carried the baby to full-term. Her child was the great singer Ethel Waters. I have met other people who were conceived when their mothers were raped. The question becomes, "Is the value of a human life determined by whether the mother and father were in love when the child was conceived?" I am convinced that if your mother and father got a divorce the day after you were conceived, that does not make you any less valuable. The value of a human life has nothing to do with whether or not the mother or father was in love or out of love.

A rape is a horrible degradation of human life. Rape is absolutely evil, not relatively evil. But once a human life is conceived, we are talking about a life whose value is not determined by the way it was conceived. Your value has nothing to do with your parents' attitudes toward you. Your value has everything to do with the fact that you are created in the image of God. You have value because God loves you so much that he sent his only Son Jesus to buy you back through his death on the cross. As difficult emotionally as it will be, I plead with those who have been raped and become pregnant to bear that child and not end its life.

Every time that I stand against abortion, I must declare the good news of forgiveness through Jesus Christ. There is a wonderful story in the Gospel of John that shows the forgiving attitude of Jesus. One day Jesus was teaching at the temple. A group of men came running to him, pushing a woman in front of them. Throwing her at the feet of Christ, they said to him, "We caught this woman in the act of adultery. In the law it says that we are to stone such a woman. What do you say we do, Jesus?" He bent down and wrote in the dirt. The men pressured him for a response.

Jesus stood up, looked the men in the face and said, "The one among you who has never committed a sin"—in other words, the one among you who has never had a desire to commit this sin—"you go ahead and throw the first stone." Then Jesus bent back down and continued writing in the dirt. The men left, one by one, beginning with the oldest. After they had all departed, Jesus stood up, looked the woman in the face, and said, "Woman, where are your accusers? Have none of them condemned you?" She said, "No one, Lord." Jesus said, "Neither do I condemn you. Go and be free of your life of sin."

That woman came to Christ guilty, but Jesus was not there to condemn. Jesus was there informing her that he would one day absorb in his body the horrible penalty for her sin. Because of his death on the cross, she could be forgiven. Because of his death in her place, she could be free. Because she knelt before him and acknowledged her need of him, he forgave her and sent her away cleansed and free to live a new life.

Regardless of whether you've had an abortion or whether you have put a woman in a position to consider having an abortion, Jesus Christ offers you forgiveness. Three days after he died on the cross, he rose from the dead. He is alive today. He wants to live in you and in me to give us the power from within to live sexually pure lives. He wants to give us the power not to turn to that which is expedient but instead to do that which is morally right, especially when it is difficult.

Question 11. Why is life important?

Life is important because it is a good gift from the God who loves us. The heart at the center of the cosmos belongs to a God who loves you and me with a deep, caring love.

Because Gus, the ten-year-old boy mentioned above, was secure in his father's love, he was free to live a positive, uncomplaining and involved life. When you and I begin to understand that God really loves us, we are free to walk humbly with God and to stop demanding more. Demanding more breeds disappointment and discontent. To walk humbly with God frees us to thank him for his generous gifts. To walk humbly with the God who loves us builds in us positive, uncomplaining spirits. To walk humbly with God produces peace in our lives. This peace and security enables us to take the necessary risks involved in engaging life with all its challenges and unknowns.

The Hebrew prophet Micah wrote that not only did God create us to act justly, he also made us to love mercy. Mercy is compassion for people in need of forgiveness.

Max Lucado writes beautifully of the love of a father for his son (*And the Angels Were Silent* [Portland, Ore.: Multnomah Press, 1992], pp. 45, 46, 51, 52):

> Artful Eddie lacked nothing. He was the slickest of the slick lawyers. He was one of the roarers of the roaring twenties. A crony of Al Capone, he ran the gangster's dog tracks. He mastered the simple technique of fixing the race by overfeeding seven dogs and betting on the eighth. Wealth. Status. Style. Artful Eddie lacked nothing. Then why did he turn

himself in? Why did he offer to squeal on Capone? What was his motive? Didn't Eddie know the sure-fire consequences of ratting on the mob? He knew, but he made up his mind. What did he have to gain? What could society give him that he didn't have? He had money, power, prestige. What was the hitch? Eddie revealed the hitch. His son. Eddie had spent his life with the despicable. He had smelled the stench of the underground long enough. For his son, he wanted more. He wanted to give his son a name, and to give his son a name, he would have to clear his own. Eddie was willing to take a risk so that his son could have a clean slate. Artful Eddie never saw his dream come true. After Eddie squealed, the mob remembered. Two shotgun blasts silenced him forever. Was it worth it? Eddie would have been proud of Butch's appointment to Annapolis. He would have been proud at the commissioning of a World War II Navy pilot. He would have been proud as he read of his son downing five bombers in the Pacific night and saving the lives of hundreds of crewmen on the Carrier Lexington. The name was cleared. The Congressional Medal of Honor which Butch received was proof. When people say the name O'Hare in Chicago, they don't think gangsters—they think aviation heroism. And now when you say his name, you have something else to think about. Think about it the next time you fly into the airport named after the son of a gangster gone good. The son of Eddie O'Hare.

The love of a father motivated him to sacrifice his own life in order to give his son a clean name. God created us to work for the well-being of others. That is love in motion. That is compassion.

Why is life important? Because God has created us in his image, each with an innate value. Therefore, we must treat each other with an appropriate dignity. We must act justly. Why is life important? Because we were created by a God who loves each individual one of us. Therefore, it is appropriate to treat each other with compassion.

Why is life important? Because we were created to walk humbly with God. This produces a positive and uncomplaining spirit. It frees us to be involved in life. Why is life important? Because we were created to walk humbly with God through this life, through death, and out the other side to eternal life in heaven.

Although I do not know why
God allowed evil,
I do know he wants to destroy it.
That is why
there is a hell.
Although I do not know why
God allowed pain,
I do know he wants to wipe
every tear
from our eyes and give us joy
for eternity in his presence.
That is why
there is a heaven.

4

Why is there evil
in the world?

The London Times *asked the great British thinker G. K. Chesterton to write* a series of three articles answering the question, "What is the problem with the world?" Chesterton responded with a single brief letter which read, "Dear Sirs, The problem with the world quite frankly is me. Respectfully, G. K. Chesterton."

The Hebrew prophet Jeremiah wrote, "The heart is deceitful above all things and beyond cure. Who can understand it? I the LORD search the heart and examine the mind, to reward a man according to his conduct, according to what his deeds deserve" (Jeremiah 17:9-10).

Jeremiah and Chesterton agree. The problem with the world is not "out there," it's "in here." It's me. It's you. It's all of us. Jesus said, "For from within, out of men's hearts, come evil thoughts, sexual immorality, theft, murder, adultery, greed, malice, deceit, lewdness, envy, slander, arrogance and folly. All these evils come from inside and make a man 'unclean'" (Mark 7:21-23). Jesus analyzed the human dilemma as being an internal sin problem.

We can't comfort ourselves by saying "I'm not as bad as so-and-so over there." In the New Testament, James wrote, "For whoever keeps the whole law and yet stumbles at just one point is guilty of breaking all of it" (James 2:10). This analysis of the human problem disturbs me; it tells me that I am part of the problem with the world.

Question 12. Where does evil come from?

I do not know why God allowed evil, pain, suffering and death to enter the world. I do not know why he allows it to continue. Philosophers and theologians have struggled with the problem of evil and have never come up with a complete answer. I promise you I never will either. However, as a Christian I have to think about these questions.

In the first chapter of Genesis, the first book of the Bible, we read that when God created, he did a good job. The little phrase "and God saw that it was good" is repeated throughout the creation narrative. In the New Testament we read that "God is light; in him there is no darkness at all" (1 John 1:5). There is not a trace of evil in God's character; God is totally good.

But when God created, he was not a computer spewing out perfect printouts. Genesis 1:27 tells us, "So God created man in his own image, in the image of God he created him; male and female he created them." Being created in the image of God does not refer to physical resemblance, but to the fact that humans have personality, conscience and will—aspects also seen in God's character.

God is all-powerful, but he chose to partially limit his power by creating us free. To the person who objects that the gift of freedom was not worth the risk, I can only reply that if you take a person's free will away, you no longer have a person: you have a machine. God is love. When he created us, he gave us the innate ability to love him and each other. Love, in order to be real, must be freely given. If a young woman tells her boyfriend "I love you" only because his father is paying her to tell him that, that is not real love. Real love is a free choice to care for someone. If love is not the result of a free choice, it is not love.

Genesis 3 tells us how human beings chose to rebel against God. As

God had warned, the consequences of rebellion against him include evil, pain, suffering and death. In Genesis 3, when humans tell God to take a hike, he partially honors their request. He steps back from planet earth. Chaos, havoc, injustice, suffering and death fill the gap. Nature is cursed. Genetic breakdown occurs. The ripple effects pass down through the generations. Sin does not simply result in a bad mood; sin leads to death.

Jesus Christ had the problem of evil thrown in his face. His response is interesting. Luke reports:

> Now there were some present at the time who told Jesus about the Galileans whose blood Pilate had mixed with their sacrifices. Jesus answered, "Do you think that these Galileans were worse sinners than all the other Galileans because they suffered this way? I tell you, no! But unless you repent, you too will all perish. Or those eighteen who died when the tower in Siloam fell on them—do you think they were more guilty than all the others living in Jerusalem? I tell you, no! But unless you repent, you too will all perish." (Luke 13:1-5)

Notice that Jesus does not answer the "Why did God allow this to happen?" question. Instead Jesus challenges us to examine our own lives carefully and to repent of our sin.

Although I do not know why God allowed evil, I do know he wants to destroy it. That is why there is a hell. Although I do not know why God allowed pain, I do know he wants to wipe every tear from our eyes and give us joy for eternity in his presence. That is why there is a heaven. Although I do not know why God allowed suffering, I do know God is a suffering God who became human in Jesus. Although I do not know why God allowed death, I do know Jesus died on the cross to forgive you and me for our sins that lead to death. I do know Jesus rose from the dead to give us eternal life with him in heaven. He waits for us to put our trust in him.

Question 13. Why do we overlook our own responsibility for evil?

Human beings consistently dabble in self-deception in order to escape the problem of evil in their lives and in the world. Self-deception is too easy for all of us to fall into.

During the 1930s in England, Winston Churchill hammered away at his leaders, telling them that Nazi Germany was in the hands of criminals. The ruling class would not accept such an analysis. They viewed such talk as "fanatical," "alarmist" and "hysterical." If the English leaders had acknowledged the evil that was in the hearts of the Nazis, they would have been forced to realize the strong possibility of an impending war. But they preferred not to. The memories of World War I were too fresh. The deaths of loved ones and friends were too clearly etched in their minds. Nobody in England wanted to think realistically that war was possibly on the horizon; therefore, they chose self-deception. But as Hitler's forces began to conquer Europe, the English were forced to recognize that Churchill had been correct.

The Bible gives us many examples of people who fell into self-deception. Adam and Eve knew that God was a generous God. But they chose to believe the lie of Satan that God was a jealous tyrant; they chose to believe the lie that God was selfishly trying to keep the top job in the universe for himself. They knew it was a lie from experiencing God's goodness firsthand. Still they chose self-deception.

Moses confronted Aaron, who was leading the people in worshiping a golden calf. Aaron couldn't imagine how the golden calf had popped out of the fire into existence. This was clear self-deception. Aaron had molded the calf out of the melted-down jewelry the Jews had brought him.

King David was outraged that a rich man would slaughter the lamb of a poor man to feed his guests. David failed to see on his own what he had done in stealing Uriah's wife, Bathsheba, and then murdering Uriah. It took the prophet Nathan to jolt David out of his self-deception.

Peter was outraged when Jesus himself informed him that he would deny Jesus. But when the cock crowed, Peter wept bitterly because he had denied the Lord three times. He thought he was incapable of denying Christ. He was self-deceived.

We are no different. Self-deception comes easily to us. We don't lose our tempers; we have justified anger. We don't lust; we are just healthy young adults. We don't gossip; we merely share vital information with others. We're not proud; we simply have high self-esteem. Our self-deception blinds us to our need of Christ's forgiveness and help. The Bible consistently challenges us to confront our self-deception. The psalmist cried out, "Search me, O God, and know my heart; / test me and know my anxious thoughts / See if there is any offensive way in me, / and lead me in the way everlasting" (Psalm 139:23-24). The apostle John wrote, "If we claim to be without sin, we deceive ourselves and the truth is not in us" (1 John 1:8). The apostle Paul advised, "A man ought to examine himself" (1 Corinthians 11:28).

God calls us to self-examination. Constant self-examination can become neurotic. But God calls us to consistently examine ourselves as we pray, as we read the Bible and as we talk with close friends. With honesty and openness we must examine our lives. It is too easy to slither away from honestly looking at my wrongdoing; it is too easy for me to say that I was simply exaggerating when in reality I was lying. I need to turn to God and ask, "O Lord, please forgive me for lying in order to stroke my ego. Help me to draw upon you for my significance and value as a person. Help me to overcome the temptation to paint an exaggerated picture of myself in order that others might admire me."

Instead of excusing my lack of serving others as an issue of time management, I need to acknowledge my passion for comfort and my distaste for discomfort. I need to cry out, "O Lord, forgive me for being overly committed to living an untroubled life." Searching, honest confession of sin is a powerful cure for self-deception.

Question 14. Why does life without God produce evil?

Feodor Dostoyevsky wrote in *The Brothers Karamazov*, "If there is no God, everything is permissible." It takes a conscious mind to define what is right and wrong. If there is no God, then there is no conscious mind prior to the human mind. Therefore, right and wrong are the creation of the human mind. Your mind defines right and wrong one way; my mind defines right and wrong a different way. You are not right or wrong; I am not right or wrong. You are right for yourself. I am right for myself.

However, both you and I deny those notions whenever we use the words *should* or *ought* (see page 36). The words *should* and *ought* tattle on us. They reveal that we really want to live our lives as if there is a standard outside of us that we can really understand by exercising our consciences in a responsible manner.

All my atheist friends live their lives as if certain deeds are really evil. The only way those deeds can be truly evil is if there is a value of justice that is being violated. The only way justice can be a real value is if there is more to reality than matter and energy. Matter and energy cannot create values such as justice. The existence of the value of justice clearly shows us that reality is bigger than simply matter and energy. There must be some type of God to create and define the value of justice.

If there is no God, then I will never have to give an account for the way I have lived my life. If there is no all-powerful, all-knowing, holy, awesome God who stands at the end of human history, then I will never to have to answer for the decisions I made in this life. But when I begin to realize that in reality God is all-powerful, morally pure and all-knowing, then my human pride and arrogance appear for what they really are, the heights of absurdity. In place of human arrogance grow an appropriate humility, reverence and adoration for the God who is so much greater than we are, that there is no real comparison.

When God is absent from a person's perspective, evil, corruption and violence win the day. The psalmist wrote, "The fool says in his heart, / 'There is no God.' / They are corrupt, their deeds are vile; / there is no one who does good" (Psalm 14:1). If there is no God, life is cheap. If there is no God, *justice* is a relative word. When people lose their fear of God, they lose a powerful deterrent to brutal behavior.

One day you and I will stand before an all-knowing, all-seeing God to give an answer for the way we chose to live our lives. I am guilty of doing wrong. God and I know that to be a fact. God calls me to face the hard facts, to confess my sin to him and to those I have wronged, and to turn to his Son Jesus Christ for forgiveness.

It is difficult for me to confess my sin because it is humiliating. However, in order to deal with my root problem, my sinfulness, I must confess my sin and turn away from it to Christ for forgiveness. The great news of Jesus Christ is that he accepts us the way we are, he forgives us for all our sins and he offers to change us.

Question 15. What is God's answer to evil in the world?

Economists have diagnosed the problem with the world as a lack of money. Philosophers have diagnosed the problem with the world as a lack of knowledge. The scientists' diagnosis is a lack of good science. The politicians diagnosis: a lack of good government. Some have diagnosed the problem with the world as rich people. Others have diagnosed it as poor people.

Jesus Christ insists that the problem with the world goes deeper. Jesus taught that the problem with the world comes from your heart and my heart, your personality and my personality. My experience tells me that his analysis of the problem is correct. My experience also tells me that he is capable of addressing the problem like no one else.

I would like to invite my atheist, agnostic and cultural Christian friends to a hospital. There I would invite them into a room where a baby lies with its life is ebbing away due to some horrible disease. I would ask my atheist and agnostic friends, "What is your solution to the death of this child?" I would ask my cultural Christian friend, who has reduced Christianity to an ethical system based on the teachings of Jesus, "What is your solution for this child's predicament?" Ultimately, they have none. A hunk of primordial slime that evolved to a higher order is passing into oblivion. Tough luck, kid. All of reality is contained in this short—for you, very short—life.

Perhaps the atheist, the agnostic and the cultural Christian will comfort the child. Perhaps they will do something to help the child get the best medical attention possible. As a follower of Christ, I too will hold the child's hand and seek to comfort this child. I too will seek the best medical attention possible for this child. But in Jesus Christ I have found the suffering God who cares about suffering, dying people. Jesus cares so much that he went through the hell of the cross so you and I can go to heaven.

Someone may challenge me, "Cliffe, you don't know what you're talking about. What do you know about finding God in suffering and death? What do you really know about crying out to God for answers that don't seem to be there?"

Everyone's personal tragedies are their own private pain, and we can't compare them as harder or easier. But let me share an experience in my own family in which we had to depend on the faithfulness of God in the middle of terrible circumstances. This story actually belongs first of all to my brother Stuart and his wife, Mary Banks. Stuart writes:

> We have not yet resolved our thoughts or feelings, nor have we understood God's ways. Therefore, I write these thoughts before reaching any resolution of the crisis I am about to share. This was a personal, family, and community tragedy that has left many people changed. I will try to honestly communicate how my faith in God interfaced with the events as they unfolded like a terrifying storm.
>
> On September 9, 1997, at 5:35 p.m., I received a page in my office at the hospital from a good friend in our neighborhood telling me that my children had been involved in a car accident, and that I might want to come to the scene. I thanked her for notifying me and began praying, asking God to be good to my children. I didn't know which of our four children was in the accident, but I knew that my wife, Mary Banks, had driven our oldest son, William, to a piano lesson, and that David and Ann had soccer games and were to be driven there by Brian Gott, a college freshman who had been staying with us.
>
> I passed two ambulances on my way to the accident site. Thinking that they might contain my children, I turned around and followed them. The second ambulance stopped and allowed me to look in the back window. The ambulance contained my youngest son, Peter, age three. I was allowed to ride with Peter the rest of the way to the hospital.
>
> When we arrived at the emergency room, I found my son David, age nine, on an examining table with injuries obviously more serious than Peter's. Brian was across the hall in the major trauma room. Soon Mary arrived with eleven-year-old William. They had not been involved in the accident. I asked several times, "Where is Ann? Where is Ann?" Mary said the words I have dreaded more than any I have ever heard: "Ann is dead."

"What?" I asked, not believing my ears.

"Ann is dead. Ann is dead. I'm sorry, I thought you knew. I thought they had told you."

I crumpled to the ground, holding my stomach, feeling as though someone had just knocked me down.

During that first night, Brian died of his injuries. We expressed our sorrow to his parents and sister. Over the next days it became apparent that both Peter and David were suffering from seizures due to traumatic brain injuries, but their CT scans and clinical exams gradually improved.

Ann's funeral was held the Saturday after the accident. Loving, supportive friends and family surrounded us. Mary and I felt so totally violated and in such numbing pain that there was literally nothing anyone could say or do that made us feel like our lives were anything other than devastated. At the funeral service we did our best to honor our beloved Ann, and to honor our God whom we ultimately trusted, but simultaneously were now struggling to believe was both powerful and good. This was not the way I would have written the script, and if the God I thought I knew was in charge of the script, how could he possibly choose this for Ann, not to mention for her family and friends?

One and a half years later, Peter and David are recovered from their brain injuries, back in school, and thriving. Their progress has surpassed expectations and been in agreement with the many prayers of-fered on their behalf by friends around the world. Mary and I continue to struggle with our loss of Ann.

Cliffe asked me to write about what this means for our faith in Jesus Christ—how has our faith been influenced by our loss, and how has our faith influenced our response to losing our daughter?

The first memorable answer to this question came from William. I was driving him to a piano recital several months later when the "why" question came up. He said to me, "Dad, I think our family is different now. We used to think we could have anything and do anything we wanted. Now we're not as snooty as we used to be." I had not considered myself to be especially "snooty," but who does?

Another response of our family has been to be less attached to the rewards of this world. We think about heaven all the time and long to be there. Mary and I have struggled with wanting to go on and would prefer to be in heaven right away, and I think most parents who lose a child experience such feelings. We can hardly wait—but we will leave the timing to God.

We have experienced feelings of severe disappointment with God. If God treats his children like this, then can he be trusted? Does he really care about us, and does our devotion to him mean anything to him? These questions are big, and I do not have satisfactory answers. They are old questions, though, that have been asked by others who thought they knew God, only to reopen these issues when they encountered severe personal loss. But we, like Job in the Bible, are becoming more awed by how much greater than us is our God.

I feel closer to the pain and suffering of others than I used to. Those who have suffered severe loss feel a new kinship with others and a desire to do what little we can to help—even when we can't change the circumstances. There is fellowship in suffering, although initiation into this club is severe and there is no waiting list for the membership roster.

Personal encouragement from my relationship with God has come infrequently and in small doses. When it does come, however, it is a profound message that leaves me changed. Mary and I have found that holding onto the words and promises of Jesus has provided us with a solid foundation for our hope that cannot be shaken even by the fulfillment of our worst personal and family nightmare. Despite this hope, we continue to struggle with feelings of deep grief and anger. I have been forced to realize how fickle is my faith, how dependent it is on a good night's sleep and positive feedback from within my small world. More than that, I realize that my faith in God is simply a gift from him, that I am dependent on his having chosen me, and that my faith will endure only by his grace, through the loving support of the community of faith that ministers to me.

That was my brother Stuart's story a year and a half after his daughter's death. Every person's story of suffering is different, but our need of Christ within our suffering is the same. When Sharon and I learned of Ann's death, Sharon burst into tears, and I felt like someone had just stuck a knife in me. The pain only increased as we learned that our two nephews, David and Peter, were comatose in the children's intensive care unit. Disbelief and numbness followed the pain. How could this happen? Why did this happen? I experienced a deep sense of my weakness, powerlessness and inability to solve this gigantic problem. Sharon and I began to pray for Mary Banks, Stuart, William, David and Peter. In the midst of the tears, we thanked Jesus that Ann was in his presence.

While flying to Madison to be with Stuart, Mary Banks, William, David and Peter, I began to imagine what their pain must be like. When I saw them, I realized there was no way I could grasp the depth of their agony. Is there any greater pain in life than the loss of a child? I doubt it. I love Stuart, Mary Banks and William so much. How frustrating it was to see them in such pain and not be able to be much help.

The first time I saw David and Peter lying on beds in the ICU, powerful emotions swept over me. Couldn't the drivers have been more careful? Anger began to well up, followed by reminders of my own carelessness behind the wheel of a car. David's and Peter's lives hung by a thread. We prayed and prayed and prayed. Although I didn't know why God allowed the accident to occur, I did know he was with us in that ICU. I knew that Jesus loves Stuart, Mary Banks, Ann, William, David and Peter deeply. I knew Jesus was taking care of Ann. I knew he would take care of her family. But in the midst of the devastation, the seeming hiddenness and silence of God were extremely difficult to understand. There were no easy answers but plenty of raw emotion.

Misinterpreting the Bible, particularly at a time like this, is not good. There are Scriptures like Proverbs 3:1-4 that speak of God granting long life and prosperity to those who follow his teachings. How did those verses apply to my brother and sister-in-law who were living lives of integrity before God and people? Stuart had often prayed, "Lord, please be good to my precious children. Please protect and care for them." What's the deal? Why was his daughter dead and two of his sons hanging on to life by a thread?

It became clear that those verses are not ironclad promises but wise principles that, if followed, will spare us unnecessary pain. But the Bible never promises those devoted to Christ a pain-free life on earth. The book of Job is a rebuke to any overly optimistic expectation of pain-free living. In John 16:33 Jesus says, "I have told you these things so that in me you may have peace. In this world you will have trouble." I appreciate the realism of Jesus. There is much trouble, pain and sorrow in this life. In the midst of my pain I began to thank God that he has a future in heaven for Ann and a future for Stuart, Mary Banks, William, David and Peter on earth (and in heaven). This hope brought great comfort to me in the midst of intense pain and sorrow.

The answers to prayer have been miraculous. David and Peter are sound in body and spirit. Stuart, Mary Banks and William are an example to me of perseverance through pain and in the midst of the mysteries of life. I miss Ann, and I can hardly wait to see her one day in heaven. Heaven is definitely sweeter because Ann is there. My experience of Christ's love convinces me that right now Ann is in good hands. A perspective that includes eternal life in heaven helps me realize the brevity of life and how I will have eternity to get to know and enjoy Ann. The love and hope found in Jesus enable me to not turn to cynicism or bitterness. The love and hope found in Christ enable me to deal with the crushing absurdity of the death of a seven-year-old girl, my niece Ann.

A few months after Ann's death, I was speaking at the University of Arizona. A student said, "I will never love or worship the God who created a world so full of suffering and death. If I were the Creator, I would have done a much better job." That night on the phone, I put that statement before Stuart and asked for his response. Stuart replied, "To suppose that I could create a better world than God created is the height of human arrogance. Who does this student think he is?" Stuart's consistent humility before God is an example to me. His continual love for Jesus and people in the midst of excruciating pain is remarkable. His insistence on thinking clearly and deeply while acknowledging the mysteries of a spiritual relationship with Christ is a model I seek to follow. I love Stuart, Mary Banks, William, David and Peter. I hurt with them. I am so grateful they draw upon Christ for grace and strength during this time of need.

The writer of Psalm 73 struggled with why he, a servant of God, had it rough while all around him the wicked were prospering. He could find no answer until he entered the presence of God in the temple and worshiped. Then the psalmist regained an eternal perspective. He was reminded that although life is unfair, God is fair.

It is so difficult to keep those facts straight. When life is unfair, it is too easy for me to get angry with God. That is misplaced anger. Life is unfair; God is fair. Never get the two mixed up. When life is unfair, the challenge is to remember that God is big enough and good enough to bring good out of evil. When life is unfair, it is important to remember that on the Day of Judgment, Jesus Christ will right the wrongs, will make the crooked straight.

Because God is good, life will ultimately turn out good. But in the meantime, there is a lot of pain and suffering. When I learn to submit to God, to give up the control of my life to him, his peace begins to rule in my heart in the midst of the injustices of this life.

How is it with you? Are you aware of your need, and do you recognize Jesus' ability to meet your need? Will you allow that to motivate you to put your faith in Jesus Christ? When you trust in Christ, he begins to give you the power to love with a love that does not fail, to be truly sincere and to have a purity of motive that is shocking. Ask Jesus Christ to begin the process of solving your problems. Allow Christ to use you as a peacemaker in a world filled with problems.

I do not know why God allowed evil, pain, suffering and death to enter the world or why he allows it to continue. But I do know God has provided the ultimate solution: forgiveness and eternal life through putting our faith in Jesus Christ. When it comes to the problem of suffering, the bottom-line questions are, Do you have God's solution to suffering and death? Do you have Jesus Christ?

Because of our ignorance

and prejudices

it is far too easy to judge

and critique each other.

It is so difficult

to yield and submit to another.

5

Why is there disharmony in relationships?

A *young boy once asked his father, "Dad, how do wars begin?" His father* answered, "Well, take World War I as an example. It started when Germany invaded Belgium." His wife interrupted him, "Tell the boy the truth. It began because somebody was murdered." Condescendingly, the husband asked, "Who's answering this question, you or I?" The wife stormed out of the room, slamming the door behind her as hard as she could.

When the dishes stopped rattling in the cupboard and the pictures stopped bouncing on the walls, the young boy said, "Daddy, you don't have to tell me how wars start. I know now!"

Question 16. What causes strife between people?

Jesus talked about the origins of "warfare" between people when he said, "For from within, out of men's hearts, come evil thoughts, sexual immorality, theft, murder, adultery, greed, malice, deceit, lewdness, envy, slander, arrogance and folly. All these evils come from inside and make a man 'unclean'" (Mark 7:21-23; see page 53). Jesus insisted that the solution for the human dilemma was not more money, more education or more technology. He called for a radical conversion at the root of a person's being. He called for people to come to him and to put their trust in him.

Later Jesus said, "If you love me, you will obey what I command. And I will ask the Father and he will give you another Counselor to be with you forever—the Spirit of truth. The world cannot accept him, because it neither sees him nor knows him. But you know him, for he lives with you and will be in you. I will not leave you as orphans; I will come to you" (John 14:15-18).

When this spiritual transformation takes place, we will begin to love each other more and more. This love will be shown in very practical ways: in the way we speak to each other and in the way we submit to one another. Jesus wants to free us from being consumed with the question "What's in it for me?" He wants to free us to be secure in his love, consumed with the question "How can I help that person?"

It is very human to greedily grasp for more; we are most godlike when we generously give. Jesus said in John 3:16, "For God so loved the world that he gave his one and only Son." That quality of love brings real excitement to life. That Jesus-style love brings peace to a marriage relationship torn apart by disharmony and strife. When the love of Christ flows freely, a boring house turns into an exciting home. Running away from that quality of love is sheer stupidity.

I know that defending my pride and position are too high a priority in my life. That priority produces anger. That priority produces disharmony and tension. Submission to one another is God's way of producing peace and harmony in human relationships.

A woman waiting for a flight in an airport decided to pass the time by buying a book and a package of cookies. After taking a seat, she became absorbed in her book. Suddenly out of the corner of her eye she saw a man two seats away open the pack of cookies on the seat between them and take one of the cookies. Quickly she took one of the cookies out of the package for herself. He proceeded to take another cookie. Not to be outdone, she quickly grabbed another. This continued until there was only one cookie left. The gentleman broke the cookie in half, taking one half for himself. She was outraged and grabbed the other half. The man left.

She was in shock; she could not believe the man's nerve. Shortly, she boarded her flight. Once aboard, still angry at the man's audacity, she reached into her purse for a tissue. To her amazement, she found her unopened package of cookies. She learned not to judge too harshly!

Because of our ignorance and prejudices it is far too easy to judge and critique each other. It is so difficult to yield and submit to another. Yet doing this is a key ingredient in building harmony in a disintegrating world.

Question 17. Shouldn't we all be fighting for our personal rights rather than submitting?

We all have a God-given drive to preserve our own lives. There is nothing wrong with that drive. Part of what motivates me to put my faith in Jesus is his promise of eternal life for me. That is not a crass selfishness. It is rather an affirmation of the value of life as a gift from God. However, my sin puts a spin on the basic, God-given drive to preserve my life. My selfishness motivates me to perform only what is good for myself.

Toddlers scream, "Mine, mine!" Adults scream, "My rights, my rights." Adults merely devise more sophisticated ways of getting what they want. By contrast, Paul wrote that love is "not self-seeking" (1 Corinthians 13:5). In fact the entire thirteenth chapter of 1 Corinthians describes love from God's perspective. It tells us that love does not selfishly demand its way, its rights, its wants. Love does not demand that I win all the time; love is primarily concerned with the well-being of the loved one. Love is not rude. Love motivates us to respect and honor because love opens our eyes to the high value of God and people.

Love Jesus-style means to give, to serve, and to sacrifice. Jesus loved, not just in theory, but in action. He sacrificed his life on the cross so that you and I might have eternal life. Jesus taught an amazing paradox: "Whoever finds his life will lose it, and whoever loses his life for my sake will find it" (Matthew 10:39). My love for God will be shown as I seek first to do the will of God. My love for people will be shown in my concern for the welfare of others.

Human beings respect what they value highly. Whom or what do you and I value highly? God values people and asks us to value them too. C. S. Lewis wrote in *The Weight of Glory* ([Grand Rapids, Mich.: Eerdmans, 1977], pp. 14-15):

> It is a serious thing to remember that the dullest and most uninteresting person you talk to may one day be a creature which, if you saw it now, you would be strongly tempted to worship or else a horror and a corruption such as you now meet, if at all, only in a nightmare. All day long, we are, in some degree, helping each other to one or other of these destinations. It is in the light of these overwhelming possibilities, it is with the awe and the circumspection proper to them, that we should conduct all our dealings with one another, all friendships, all loves, all play, all politics. There are no ordinary people.

The apostle Paul tells us to "submit to one another out of reverence for Christ" (Ephesians 5:21). Submission to one another is a result of respecting Jesus Christ. Secure in Christ's love and call on my life, I am free to yield to others.

Yielding to others is difficult for me. Too much of my significance and security in life is based on getting my way. Yielding to another person is always difficult, but that is what Christ calls us to. Two things are hard on the heart: running up stairs and running down people. The Bible says, "Do not let any unwholesome talk come out of your mouths, but only what is helpful for building others up according to their needs, that it may benefit those who listen" (Ephesians 4:29).

Paul expanded on the theme of submission by saying, "Wives, submit to your husbands as to the Lord. For the husband is the head of the wife as Christ is the head of the church, his body, of which he is the Savior" (Ephesians 5:22-23). While this statement of Paul irritates many people, he issued an equally strong call for husbands to set aside their own selfishness: "Husbands, love your wives, just as Christ loved the church and gave himself up for her, to make her holy, cleansing her by the washing with water through the word" (Ephesians 5:25-26). Both of these examples of submission must be seen in the context of the introductory admonition to "submit to one another out of reverence for Christ."

Submission is not blindly following the blind. Submission is not propping up evil or abuse. Submission is not encouraging the irresponsibility of others. Submission is showing honor, giving respect and going beyond the call of duty.

The Greek word for "submit" is *hupotassō*. It means "to draw up alongside and voluntarily complete." To love my wife as Christ loved the church means to serve her even as Jesus served his disciples by washing their feet. Voluntarily completing another person and serving another human being are not natural instincts for us. They are qualities that Jesus Christ wants to grow in our lives.

When some people walk into a room, they have the attitude *Here I am*. When Jesus walked into a room, he had the attitude *There you are*. Love is shown in the way we take a genuine interest in other people, reach for them and initiate interaction.

To submit means to show honor, to give respect, to go beyond the call of duty as a servant. That is very unnatural for people obsessed with their own personal rights. But it is the way of Christ. It is the way God wants to heal sick, broken relationships.

Laurie was in sixth grade. One day her teacher, Mrs. Lake, informed the class that it was the day of the student-parent-teacher conferences. On the blackboard in alphabetical order was a list of all the families. Laurie's name was on the list, but it really didn't matter. She knew that in spite of the reminder letters and the phone calls, her parents would not show up. Her father was an alcoholic, and his drinking that year had become horrendous. Many nights Laurie would fall asleep to the sounds of her father shouting, her mother sobbing, the doors slamming and the pictures rattling on the walls. The previous Christmas Laurie and her younger sister had saved their baby-sitting money in order to buy their father a shoeshine kit. They had wrapped it carefully and tied a bow around it. They watched in stunned silence as their father opened the gift and then threw it against the wall with such force that it broke into three pieces.

On the day of the conferences, Laurie watched all day long as proud parents patted their children on the back, gave them hugs and went out into the hallway to meet with Mrs. Lake. Laurie wondered what it would feel like to have her parents greet her at the classroom door.

After all the other students had had their turn, Mrs. Lake opened the door and motioned for Laurie to join her in the hall. Embarrassed by the absence of her parents, Laurie sat in the chair and stared at the floor. Mrs. Lake moved her chair close to Laurie. She took Laurie's hand, lifted her chin, and looked deeply into her eyes. Mrs. Lake began, "First of all, you need to know how much I love you." Laurie was startled. She had not received many loving words in her life. Mrs. Lake continued, "Second, you need to know that it is not your fault that your parents are not here today." Laurie was amazed. No one had ever talked to her like this before. Mrs. Lake continued, "Third, you deserve a conference whether your parents are here or not. You deserve to hear how well you are doing and how wonderful I think you are."

In the next few minutes Mrs. Lake and Laurie had their own conference. At some point in that conference, Laurie heard the voice of hope in her heart. She began to realize for the first time in her life that she was actually lovable. During that conference, Mrs. Lake loved, encouraged and brought healing and hope to a sixth-grade girl.

Love Jesus-style is a love that initiates. It is a love that reaches for the unloved. It is all too human to love the beautiful and popular people. It is godlike to love all people, including the unattractive and the unpopular. God sends the rain on the righteous and the unrighteous. He loves those who are in open rebellion against him. His love is not rooted in the kindness of somebody else; his love is rooted in his own character. Jesus Christ wants to produce that type of loving character in you and me.

Question 18. Shouldn't I be in control of my life?

God chose to create us with free will. There are negative repercussions in my life due to my irresponsible decisions. There are also negative repercussions in my life due to the irresponsible decisions of others. I don't like that. Therefore, I struggle to control as many of the circumstances of my life as I can.

I admit that I love to be in control. The problem is that if I insist upon being in control, I'm never going to know God. If I'm a control freak, I will never have a deep marriage relationship nor will I ever have satisfying relationships with my children. If I feel the need to control everybody, and if I think that I can control my life and even control God, I am deluding myself.

One of the most pathetic examples of that delusion was when Ernest Hemingway blew his brains out so that he could be in control of the one thing that he knew he probably wouldn't otherwise be able to control—when he would die. So he seized control with a gun and ended his life.

How sad! How empty! And the irony is that as I give up control to Jesus Christ, as I stop trying to manipulate people or control people, but learn to love and respect people in humility, as I learn to be a humble husband who serves instead of one who has to be in control, I am surprised by real joy, by real peace. Yes, I am called to lead—there is no question about that—but not to control or manipulate.

If you play the control game, you will be plagued by stress. However, as you and I surrender the control to Christ, and as we learn to respect and love each other and not to control each other, we are surprised by a quality of relationship with Christ and with friends and family that is truly exciting and satisfying.

In the October 25, 1997, *Wisconsin State Journal,* William Wineke told the story of someone whose dreams were shattered but who learned to yield control to God:

> When Green Bay Packers tight end, Mark Chmura, picked up a newspaper one spring day in 1995 and learned he was likely to be replaced by Keith Jackson, of the Miami Dolphins, he was hardly pleased.
>
> "Finally, I had put it all together—strength, speed and skills—and 1995 was supposed to be my year," Chmura writes in the current issue of *Guideposts* magazine.
>
> "But just when I thought my job as a starter was secure, I was reading

in the paper that the Packers were offering my position to Keith Jackson." Some players might have gone out and gotten drunk; other might have whined to the press. Chmura says he prayed.

"I don't understand why you are testing me," I prayed. "Help me show the Packers I can do the job. Help me stay in football and take care of my family." The rest of the story is, of course, history. Jackson and Chmura became colleagues, not enemies, and their teamwork helped win the Super Bowl. But, Chmura continued, in the beginning he continued to pray for strength to treat his potential rival with respect.

"I knew I would have to work with him, and I wanted to start off right. No matter what happened, I wanted to be proud of the way I conducted myself.

"I said a short prayer asking for strength, walked over and introduced myself. 'Welcome to Green Bay,' I said, shaking his hand." During the season, Chmura said, "The press kept at it all season, trying to stir up a rivalry between Keith and me.

"They begged our coach, 'Give us some dirt. The two of them can't be getting along. It's impossible.' Well, Keith and I showed everyone it was possible—something, of course, God had known all along. We both sacrificed playing time, but it was obvious that sharing the position was a huge plus for the team."

Now that Jackson has retired, Chmura says he learned something from the experience.

"Now I know why God tests us. Not so he can see what we are made of, but so we can see what we're made of, and what we can accomplish with his help. The answer is simple: Anything—in football and life."

In order to build teamwork on the Green Bay Packers, Mark Chmura had to let go of the position and status he wanted for himself and thought he deserved. Both Chmura and Keith Jackson chose to focus on mutual respect instead of getting what each wanted for himself.

Confronted by whatever blocks our getting what we want, you and I can yell, kick, scream, manipulate, harbor anger and hatred. Confronted by obstacles to what we think we should have, you and I can throw up our hands, give up and give in with a fatalistic attitude. But Christ calls us to a better response than any of those. Jesus calls us to submit and yield control to him.

James the half-brother of Jesus wrote, "God opposes the proud but gives grace to the humble. Submit yourselves, then, to God" (James 4:6-7). The apostle Peter, quoting the same Old Testament Scripture, wrote, "God opposes the proud but gives grace to the humble. Humble yourselves, therefore, under God's mighty hand, that he may lift you up in due time. Cast all your anxiety on him because he cares for you" (1 Peter 5:5-7).

How many proud people does it take to screw in a light bulb? Only one. The proud person holds onto the light bulb and waits for the world to revolve around him! If I am proud and refuse to submit to God, I will be at war with him, for God is the ruler of the universe. But if I submit, I will experience peace with God. He is the Creator and I am a creature. Submitting to him is the only way for us to live in harmony.

Question 19. What is Christ's solution for disharmony in relationships?

God has created and defined real love. Paul wrote that love "does not envy" (1 Corinthians 13:4). Envy is competitiveness gone rotten. Envy is a feeling of discontent and ill will because of another's advantages, possessions or successes. Envy motivates us to resent others simply because they have something we desire. Envy is often the root of sin, for envy drives us to play God. We are even envious of God's position! Therefore, we want to seize his position and act as if we are God. The sad thing is that envy drives us away from God and away from others. Envy shoots at others and wounds itself.

There is a fable that tells of the devil crossing the Libyan desert. He met some demons who were tempting a holy hermit. The demons tried to seduce the hermit through lust, doubts and fears. But they repeatedly failed. The holy man was unmovable. The devil stepped forward and said to his demons, "Your methods are too crude. Allow me a chance." Going up to the holy man, the devil asked, "Have you heard the news? Your brother has been made bishop of Alexandria." A scowl of envy quickly clouded the peaceful face of the holy man.

The cure for envy is to learn to rejoice in the goodness of God. The cure includes learning to be content in who God has made you and the position he has placed you in. Part of the cure for envy is to work for, to pray for and to rejoice over the success of others.

First Corinthians 13:4 also says that love is patient. Patience is love under pressure. Patience is love that continues when the reasons to continue grow fewer in number. Patience grows as my view of God and myself becomes more accurate.

When I begin to understand that God is at work within people's lives, I don't have to be impatient. When I understand that I am a sinner, I am more patient with fellow sinners. Because of an inaccurate view of myself, I forget how patient God has been with me. Reminded of God's patience with me, and my own sinfulness, I am free to grow in patience.

Patience also grows as we learn to bear with one another in love. To bear with one another means to give each other room to grow. To bear with one another means to allow people the room to develop into the unique persons that God intends them to be. To bear with each other means that we refuse to control each other; instead we want to empower each other to become all that God wants us to be.

People often accuse Christians of not loving each other as we should and as Christ taught us. Sadly, these accusations are often true; there is disharmony in many relationships, including relationships among Christians. But Christ's solution is still the same.

A very diverse group of people in Ephesus put their faith in Christ. They received from Jesus the free gift of eternal life; they allowed the Holy Spirit to live within them; they became God's workmanship. Paul explained how they were to love one another: He told them to be completely humble and gentle. He called them to be patient, bearing with one another in love. He urged them to make every effort to keep the unity of the Spirit in the bond of peace. He admonished them to put off the old self that was being corrupted by its deceitful desires. He challenged them to put on the new self, created to be like God in true righteousness and holiness. He taught them to put off falsehood and speak truthfully to one another. This is what it means to love one another in the church.

No church is perfect. If I found the perfect church and joined it, it would no longer be perfect. The church is Christ's hospital. If you go to a hospital and find only people who are already well, you know the hospital is not performing its function. If you go to church and find a group of "perfect" people, you know the church is not performing its function.

The church is to be like a hospital. In that hospital Christ is helping proud people become humble. He's helping harsh people become gentle. He's assisting impatient people to become patient. He's molding narrow, judgmental people into accepting and loving ones. In his church Christ is changing people who are consumed with competition, rivalry, envy and jealousy into people who are real team players, people who work for peace and harmony. In his family of faith Christ is changing people who are scarred by their old warped natures into new people, people who are becoming more and more like Jesus in the way they live their lives. In his church Christ is calling men and women to speak the truth to each other in love. In his church Christ is changing imperfect lovers into real lovers. What an exciting spiritual pilgrimage!

What is Christ's solution to the disharmony and tension in our relationships? He wants to release us from the straitjacket of our self-centeredness and free us to really love one another. Jesus wants to change us from people who walk into a room with a *Here I am* attitude into people who walk into a room with a *There you are* attitude.

What is Christ's solution for the disharmony and tension in our relationships? Jesus calls us to put our faith in him and to allow his Holy Spirit to live within us. As we surrender to the Holy Spirit and allow him to grip our lives, we will build others up instead of shredding them into little pieces. As we follow Jesus Christ, tension and disharmony in our relationships will be replaced by real love and peace.

When we ask Jesus Christ

for forgiveness,

he indeed forgives us.

Our feelings are not

the final

authority;

he is the authority.

6

Who needs forgiveness?

Have *you ever heard of a baseball umpire who called out, "Strike three!* You're out! But because you're such a nice guy, I'll give you three more chances"? I doubt it. Have you ever heard of a porpoise forgiving a shark for eating his porpoise friend? I doubt that too. You and I live in a "dog-eat-dog" world, not a "dog-forgive-dog" world. I have a T-shirt that says, "It's a dog-eat-dog world, and I'm wearing Milkbone underwear."

When we kill, we are most like beasts. When we hold a grudge, we are most like humans. But when we forgive, we are most like God.

Question 20. What is real forgiveness?

To forgive means to send away, to let go and to give up. To forgive means to give up my right to hate you for the dastardly thing you did to me. To forgive means to agree to live with the consequences of another's sin without seeking revenge. It means not being filled with bitterness but instead being filled with God's love.

The person who forgives always sacrifices. If we forgive someone, we are agreeing to absorb the hurt and the loss. We are refusing to take a pound of flesh out of the person who took the pound of flesh out of us. Forgiveness is never cheap and easy; it always demands sacrifice.

When Jesus offers you and me forgiveness, it is not a cheap forgiveness. It cost him his life. When he bled and died on the cross, he was absorbing in his body the just penalty we deserve for our wrongdoing. He willingly forgives you and me because he wants us to enter a spiritual relationship with the living God and to enjoy that relationship for eternity. The cost of forgiveness is great. The motivating factor is the deep love that Christ has for you and me.

Although forgiveness is generously offered, it is impossible for two estranged parties to come back together again unless at least one asks for forgiveness and the other grants it. If I steal your car, you might choose to offer me forgiveness. If I see nothing wrong in stealing your car, I see no need to humble myself and ask you for forgiveness. Although you offer me forgiveness, reconciliation between you and me is impossible, for I refuse to acknowledge that I have done anything wrong. You can offer me forgiveness day in and day out, but reconciliation between you and me does not take place because I am unwilling to humble myself and ask you for forgiveness.

To forgive another person means to accept what has happened, to accept the apology and to pledge to live in the present and in the future, not in the past. To forgive is to take a step of faith. It is to trust that at the end of human history, when all of us stand before God, he will judge each one of us justly. Therefore I do not have to judge another person; I can trust God to judge fairly and justly.

God can offer you and me forgiveness day in and day out. But reconciliation between God and us will never take place until we humbly ask him for forgiveness. Forgiveness is not cheap and easy; it cost Christ dearly to offer it to us. However, forgiveness does not operate until you and I ask Christ for it. When we ask him for forgiveness, he promises to purify us from all wrongdoing.

Don't attempt to change God into some type of loving cosmic ooze.

Don't hide behind an illusion because you fear the judgment. Acknowledge God's infinite knowledge, the mystery of his greatness, the amazing mercy that flows from his being. Humble yourself and ask Christ for forgiveness. Based on his authority, know that you are forgiven. Rejoice in the fact that you are reconciled to God. Rejoice that you are now his child. Rejoice that he has forgiven you, that he is with you and that you will live with him for eternity.

Question 21. If God is forgiving, why do we try to cover up our sins?
The thought that I will have to stand before God one day and give an answer for the moral decisions I made in my life is very intimidating. The judgment of God scares me. Therefore, I often try to cover up my sin and seek to create an illusion of my own goodness. Then I become confident that God will be very impressed with this wonderful self I have created.

Often I try to cover up my sins because I am something of a moral perfectionist. To admit failure in any area of life is difficult for me, but to admit failure in the moral realm is downright embarrassing. So I cover up to make sure that I spare myself the embarrassment of self-judgment.

I am also afraid of the judgment of other people. God has given all of us a strong desire to be liked. None of us appreciates being rejected by others. In order to minimize others' rejecting us, we put our best foot forward. We do not find it easy to confess to others that we have done wrong. We understand how fickle and judgmental people can be. Therefore it is much easier and more comfortable to cover up our sin.

Yet we human beings insist upon covering up our sins. That is why the apostle John wrote, "If we claim to be without sin, we deceive ourselves and the truth is not in us. If we confess our sins, he is faithful and just and will forgive us our sins and purify us from all unrighteousness. If we claim we have not sinned, we make him out to be a liar and his word has no place in our lives" (1 John 1:8-10).

Once we have the motivation to cover up, the deed is very easy. We compare our insignificant misdeeds to the acts of criminals featured on the six o'clock news in order to convince ourselves and others that we really are morally superior specimens. We don't compare ourselves to Mother Teresa or to Jesus. That would be too embarrassing and too revealing. Instead, we compare ourselves to those who are committed to ethnic cleansing, to Nazis and the Ku Klux Klan. We compare ourselves to those who commit heinous crimes on the streets of our cities.

Once we have the motivation, the cover-up is so easy. We blame our environment and others for the wrong that we do. We are like little Ted. His mother was the pianist in the church. She gave him a sandwich to eat during the service to keep him quiet. While the minister was preaching, little Ted hurled his sandwich at the minister. The minister, seeing the flying projectile out of the corner of his eye, ducked just in time.

After the service, Ted's distraught mother asked him, "Why did you throw the sandwich at the minister? Don't you realize how wrong that was?" Ted's simple answer was, "The minister talks too much."

A visiting professor at Harvard asked his history class a question: "Who was responsible for the Holocaust?" The unanimous decision of the Harvard history class was that no one was responsible for the Holocaust. We are simply slaves of our genetic makeup and the influences of our environment. We are all victims; none of us is responsible for the evil that we do.

That is a cover-up, for in reality we are not simply victims. We are created in the image of God. Part of his image includes a free will. Because we are free, we are responsible for the decisions we make. We might enjoy blaming others, but the responsibility for our deeds falls on our shoulders.

When we try to cover up our sins, we actually try to change the character of God. It is fashionable to view God as some cosmic ooze we call love. God is too all-forgiving and possibly too forgetful to judge anyone, we think. But Jesus revealed that God is hardly forgetful; he is all-knowing. Jesus revealed that although God offers all of us forgiveness, that forgiveness cannot operate until we ask him to forgive us and accept his mercy.

Question 22. Why is it so hard to forgive?
Paul wrote that love "keeps no record of wrongs" (1 Corinthians 13:5).

One reason that I keep a record of wrongs is to be prepared for when you confront me with my wrongdoing. When you confront me with something I have done wrong, I can be quick to remind you of the wrong you have done. We want to maintain our position of moral superiority. We feel the need to be able to rub a person's face in the wrongs committed in the past in order to maintain our superiority when we are caught red-handed.

Keeping a record of wrongs also gives us a reason to hold a grudge against another person. There is something very natural about seeking revenge. It is an attempt to even the score, to eke out some type of justice in this unfair world. But seeking revenge never works. It traps us in a prison of bitterness and hatred.

One of the reasons it is so difficult to forgive is that when we forgive someone for the horrible thing that they did, we are no longer in a position of superiority. If you do something wrong to me and I do not forgive you, I enjoy going about my life with a clear understanding of how superior I am to you, you rotten person. But when I forgive you, I am no longer superior to you. We are even. Giving up that superior feeling is difficult.

Another reason for the difficulty of forgiving is that forgiveness always necessitates sacrifice. God offers you and me forgiveness, but that forgiveness is not cheap and easy. The forgiveness God offers us involved the sacrifice of his only Son on a cross. Whenever forgiveness takes place, someone absorbs the pain of the wrongdoing and frees the other person from the rightful consequences of his or her wrongdoing.

If you forgive me for taking a hunk of meat out of you, you are giving up your right to take a hunk of meat out of me. You are absorbing the pain, the loss. You forgive because you realize that relationships are more important than getting even, but this invariably involves sacrifice.

One of the greatest revelations of the Bible is that the just God is in the business of forgiving people who have done wrong. When God forgives us, he does not hold our past against us. He accepts the past; he accepts the apology. And he builds a relationship with us in the present and in the future. He does not rub our faces in the past. This frees us to enjoy life with great fulfillment and spontaneity.

If any of our relationships are going to grow deep, we must forgive each other. When you get to know any person well enough, you will discover that person has a problem with wrongdoing. When that person hurts you, you will have to make a decision. You will either retreat from the person and condemn the relationship to superficiality, or you will forgive the person and allow the relationship to deepen.

If you get to know me well enough, there will be things you will have to forgive me for. And if I get to know you intimately enough, there will be things I will need to forgive you for. Forgiveness allows us as human beings to progress beyond superficial relationships and to deeply care for each other. Forgiveness is the practical side of accepting people as they are. If I refuse to forgive, it means that I have never genuinely asked God to forgive me.

The apostle Peter once came up to Jesus and asked, "Lord, how many times shall I forgive my brother when he sins against me? Up to seven times?" Jesus answered, "I tell you, not seven times, but seventy-seven times" (Matthew 18:21-22). Some translations say "seventy times seven."

Then Jesus told the parable of the unmerciful servant (Matthew 18:23-35). A king wanted to settle accounts with his servants. A man who owed him millions of dollars was brought before him. The king said to the man, "Pay up." The servant fell on his knees and asked that the king be patient with him for he did not have the money to repay the debt. The king took pity on him, canceled the debt, and let him go.

As the servant was leaving, he met a fellow servant who owed him a few dollars. He grabbed his fellow servant and began to choke him. "Pay back what you owe me now!" he demanded. His fellow servant fell on his knees before him and begged him, "Please be patient with me, and I will pay it all back." But the servant refused to be patient. Instead he had his fellow servant thrown into prison for a small debt.

When the other servants saw this, they ran to the king and said, "Oh, king, do you remember the servant whose large debt you canceled? Well, he just threw a fellow servant into prison for a few dollars' debt." The king called the first servant in. He said, "You wicked servant! I canceled all that debt of yours because you begged me to. Shouldn't you have had mercy on your fellow servant just as I had on you?" In anger the king had the servant thrown into prison until he could pay back all he owed.

Then Jesus said some of the most sobering words in the Bible. "This is how my heavenly Father will treat each of you unless you forgive your brother from your heart" (Matthew 18:35).

If I refuse to forgive another human being, it shows that I have no understanding of all that God has forgiven me. If I refuse to forgive someone else, it shows that I have a hardness that is committed to keeping score and getting even.

Gabriel García Márquez, in his book *Love in the Time of Cholera,* shows how a marriage disintegrates over a bar of soap. It was the wife's responsibility to keep the soap dish full. One day, in an exaggerated tone of voice, the husband complains that he has been unable to bathe with soap for one week because the soap dish is empty. She denies the oversight. Their pride is at stake. Neither is willing to apologize. For seven months they sleep in separate rooms and eat in silence. Even when they grow old, they are careful not to bring up the issue of the soap. To talk about that soap would lead to opening up the old wounds again.

How can a bar of soap ruin a marriage? Relationships are ruined when we refuse to say, "Stop. This standoff must come to an end. I am sorry for what I did wrong. Would you please forgive me?" Only forgiveness can halt the deterioration of a relationship.

At the center of the good news of Jesus is the message that I will never be able to earn or deserve God's forgiveness and his gift of eternal life. God's forgiveness and eternal life are free gifts which he offers me through Jesus Christ. In order to accept those gifts, I must humble myself. In humility I must ask for forgiveness and put my faith in Jesus Christ. It is that appropriate humility and understanding of all that I have been forgiven that is the foundation for my forgiving others.

Real love keeps no record of wrongs. To forgive is to act like a human being created in the image of God. To seek revenge is to act like an animal. Christ calls you and me to rise above acting like animals and instead to act like the wonderful human beings God created us to be.

Question 23. Since forgiving is so difficult, how can we do it?

In light of how difficult it is, how can we go about forgiving? First, we must separate the person from the action. C. S. Lewis wrote in *Mere Christianity* ([New York: Macmillan, 1952], p. 106):

> Christianity does not want us to reduce by one atom the hatred we feel for cruelty and treachery. We ought to hate them. Not one word of what we have said about them needs to be unsaid. But it does want us to hate them in the same way in which we hate things in ourselves: being sorry the man should have done such things, and hoping, if it is anyway possible, that somehow, sometime, somewhere, he can be cured and made human again.

I hate the wrongdoing I do, but I affirm my value as a person created in the image of God. I hate the evil other people do, but I affirm their value as human beings; therefore, I forgive them.

When we forgive, we are taking a step of faith. Paul wrote, "Do not take revenge, my friends, but leave room for God's wrath, for it is written: 'It is mine to avenge; I will repay,' says the Lord" (Romans 12:19). When I forgive, I am trusting that God is a better judge than I am. I am too emotionally involved in a given situation, and my knowledge of the facts is too partial, for me to be able to judge fairly. Forgiveness is an act of faith by which I give up my position to judge and leave it to God, because I know that he is a far more reliable judge than I am.

We are also motivated to forgive when we remember that the ground at the foot of the cross of Christ is level ground. The only reason a murderer or rapist will be in heaven is because Jesus Christ died on the cross for their sin. The only reason that I will be in heaven is because Jesus Christ died on the cross for my sin.

In light of this fact, it is self-righteous arrogance for me to refuse to forgive you. We all depend upon Christ for mercy. When we really accept his forgiveness, we realize we don't deserve it. We are the recipients of an incredible gift. Parading around holding grudges and seeking revenge shows that I do not understand how much God has forgiven me. I am still playing the game of one-upsmanship, of moral superiority. When a person's hardness and selfishness have been melted by the forgiveness of Christ, that person is free to genuinely forgive others.

Paul was one of eleven children. He grew up in a home marked by violence and abuse. When he was five, his mother died. His father spanked him for crying over her death. When he was eleven, he shot a man in an attempted holdup. While in prison, he asked Christ for forgiveness, placed his faith in Christ and asked Jesus to heal him and change him. Upon his release from prison, he married a woman and they had a little girl.

One Christmas money was scarce. Unable to handle the tension, Paul exploded at his wife and little girl. His daughter ran out of the house, found an old shoe box, and wrapped it in pretty Christmas paper. She tied a bow around it and handed it to her daddy. He opened it and flew into another rage. He shouted at her, "Don't you know better than to give an empty present to a person! What a foolish thing to do!" Tears began to flow down his little daughter's face. She blurted out, "It's not empty, Daddy. I filled it with kisses for you."

Paul's heart melted. He knelt with his wife and daughter and asked them to forgive him. Then he asked God to forgive him and to give him another chance as a husband and a father.

Some of us are convinced that at best life is an empty shoe box. Others of us have only experienced life as a box filled with hatred, bitterness and revenge. But in reality, life is a gift from God filled with his forgiveness, love and salvation. Jesus calls you and me to follow him. Jesus calls us to turn away from bitterness and revenge and to turn to him allowing him to fill our emptiness with his love, forgiveness and presence.

Question 24. What is the difference between real and false guilt?

God has created you and me with an alarm system. It's a moral alarm system that we call "conscience." If a person lacks that moral alarm system, that person is not totally human. For if a person never experiences guilt, that person is capable of committing atrocities and feeling no remorse, no guilt over it. Guilt is a device God has placed within you and me to steer us away from evil and to steer us toward doing what is good and true. There is such a thing as true, healthy guilt.

The Gospel of John tells a powerful story of guilt, accusation and forgiveness:

> At dawn he [Jesus] appeared again in the temple courts, where all the people gathered around him, and he sat down to teach them. The teachers of the law and the Pharisees brought in a woman caught in adultery. They made her stand before the group and said to Jesus, "Teacher, this woman was caught in the act of adultery. In the Law Moses commanded us to stone such women. Now what do you say?" They were using this question as a trap in order to have a basis for accusing him.
>
> But Jesus bent down and started to write on the ground with his finger. When they kept on questioning him, he straightened up and said to them, "If any one of you is without sin, let him be the first to throw a stone at her." Again he stooped down and wrote on the ground.
>
> At this, those who heard began to go away one at a time, the older ones first, until only Jesus was left, with the woman still standing there. Jesus straightened up and asked her, "Woman, where are they? Has no one condemned you?"
>
> "No one, sir," she said.
>
> "Then neither do I condemn you," Jesus declared. "Go now and leave your life of sin." (John 8:2-11)

For the teachers of the Law and the Pharisees, this woman was not a person. They had reduced the woman to an exhibit. They were using her to try to trap Jesus in order to accuse him.

Notice that when Jesus responded to the accusers, he did not question God's moral law. He did not overlook the sinful act of adultery the woman had committed. He did not say, "It's all right, ladies and gentlemen, morality is relative. It really doesn't matter what this woman has done. Stop being so uptight, guys." Jesus did not question or minimize God's moral absolutes.

Also notice that Jesus did not question God's ability to distinguish between right and wrong. Nor did Jesus question God's right and responsibility to judge fairly. But what Jesus did question was the right and the ability of those men to judge the woman. Jesus was essentially trying to point out to them, "You are all sinners. Your motives are twisted. Your knowledge of the situation is limited. You are inadequate judges."

Notice the response of the woman. When Jesus asked her, "Has no one condemned you?" she responded, "No one, sir." Her respect for Jesus was deep and genuine. Jesus responded, "Neither do I condemn you. Go now and leave your life of sin."

The woman came to Christ guilty. She realized it. The men came to Christ guilty also. They did not realize it.

When we feel guilt, we should not quickly dismiss it. Instead, we should allow our moral alarm system to wake us up to the fact that something is not right in our lives. The alarm system called guilt should motivate us to examine our lives carefully to find out what is indeed wrong. Once we discover what we have done wrong, we should turn to Jesus Christ for forgiveness.

However, there is also a false guilt. After we have asked Jesus to forgive us for our sin, if we continue to experience guilt, that is a wrong type of guilt. When we ask Jesus Christ for forgiveness, he indeed forgives us. Our feelings are not the final authority; he is the authority. If we continue to feel guilty, we need to surrender those feelings to the Lord Jesus Christ. We need to thank him for the reality that indeed he has forgiven us.

Satan uses false guilt to neutralize us and to drain our limited resources. John wrote in Revelation, "For the accuser of our brothers, who accuses them before our God day and night, has been hurled down" (12:10). Satan is identified as the one who delights in heaping accusations upon us. That has the sorry effect of making us feel useless and ineffective. Those voices have a way of convincing us that we are too far gone for God to be able to use us. Nothing could be further from the truth.

In the first chapter of the Gospel of Matthew there is a list of the genealogy of Jesus which includes women with past records that people could use to disqualify them. Tamar and Rahab were prostitutes; Bathsheba had committed adultery with David. But all of those women had turned to God for mercy. He forgave them, and he used them in great ways. False guilt is a tool of the devil to make us feel worthless. Because of the authority of Jesus Christ, you and I are forgiven when we ask him for forgiveness.

> Jesus said, "If you hold to my teaching, you are really my disciples. Then you will know the truth, and the truth will set you free." They [his opponents] answered him, "We are Abraham's descendants and have never been slaves of anyone. How can you say that we shall be set free?" Jesus replied, "I tell you the truth, everyone who sins is a slave to sin. Now a slave has no permanent place in the family, but a son belongs to it forever. So if the Son sets you free, you will be free indeed." (John 8:31-36)

Everyone who sins is a slave to sin. But when you meet Jesus, you will know the truth, and the truth will set you free. And once the Son of God sets you free, you will be free indeed!

When you have
a big vision of God,
you make a big commitment
to him.
When you have
an accurate understanding
of Christ's greatness,
it is reasonable
to make a total sacrifice
to him.
You don't make
a radical commitment
to a small, provincial God.
You do make
a radical commitment
to the Creator of
the heavens and the earth
who loves you.

7

Who is God and who is Jesus?

T*he clouds began to gather. The drizzle began to fall. Suddenly a Michigan*
State student stepped out of the crowd and said, "I'm an atheist. God, if
you really exist, it's very easy to convince me. Simply part the clouds
and shine a shaft of sunlight upon me, and I will believe. You must do
it in the next sixty seconds. Starting now: 60, 59, 58, 57, 56 . . ."

I interrupted the student's countdown and said, "Your lack of sin-
cerity reminds me of the young man who has just learned from his
girlfriend that she really loves him. But his response is simple: 'Unless
you have sex with me, I refuse to believe that you truly love me.' That
is crass manipulation. That is an example of jerking a person around.
You can't treat God that way any more than you should treat people
that way. You must allow people to reveal their love to you as they
choose. You must have the humility to allow God to reveal himself to
you as he chooses, not as you stipulate."

Once a person realizes that it is most reasonable to believe that
God exists, the next logical question is, "Who is this God? What is this

God like?" It is at this point that we all hit a brick wall. None of us is intelligent enough to figure out God. It is only the arrogant who claim to be smart enough to be able to figure out God on their own.

But this limitation should not discourage us from trying to find out who God is, because the same thing is true in every human relationship. I am not smart enough to figure out any person. You and I depend on each other to reveal to each other who we really are, what we really are like.

If you do not open up and speak the truth about yourself to me, I will never get to know you. Similarly, if I do not open up and reveal the truth about myself to you, you will never get to know me. In order to develop a relationship with a person, there must be open, honest communication. If one person insists upon remaining silent, or if they lie, then it is impossible to get to know them.

God has not remained silent. He has not lied to us. He has made it possible for us to get to know him. In fact, he has taken the initiative in Jesus Christ to show us who he is and help us develop a relationship with him.

Question 25. I attend a worship service every week. What more does God want?

The apostle Paul was a man in touch with reality. In the first eleven chapters of the book of Romans, Paul outlined the sinfulness of human beings, the depth of God's love for us in sending Jesus to bleed and die on a cross for our sin, and the greatness and majesty of God. At the end of Romans 11, Paul wrote this:

> Oh, the depth of the riches of the wisdom and knowledge of God! How unsearchable his judgments, and his paths beyond tracing out! Who has known the mind of the Lord? Or who has been his counselor? Who has ever given to God, that God should repay him? For from him and through him and to him are all things. To him be the glory forever! Amen. (Romans 11:33-36)

Such a paean of praise and worship is the only possible result of an accurate view of several things: human depravity, God's deep love for us, and the greatness and majesty of God. No wonder Paul went on to write:

> Therefore, I urge you, brothers, in view of God's mercy, to offer your
> bodies as living sacrifices, holy and pleasing to God—this is your spiri-
> tual act of worship. Do not conform any longer to the pattern of this
> world, but be transformed by the renewing of your mind. Then you will
> be able to test and approve what God's will is—his good, pleasing and
> perfect will. (Romans 12:1-2)

Paul's reasoning is clear. When you have a big vision of God, you
make a big commitment to him. When you have an accurate understanding of Christ's greatness, it is reasonable to make a total sacrifice
to him. You don't make a radical commitment to a small, provincial
God. You do make a radical commitment to the Creator of the heavens
and the earth who loves you.

To worship means to consider ultimately worthy. When we have a
big vision of God, we naturally worship him. To worship means to
offer one's whole self. That includes inward thoughts, feelings and
aspirations, words and deeds.

The Bible reveals that God created us to worship him and him
alone. In Exodus 20:1-7 we read the first three of the Ten Commandments:

> And God spoke all these words:
> "I am the LORD your God, who brought you out of Egypt, out of the land
> of slavery.
> You shall have no other gods before me.
> You shall not make for yourself an idol in the form of anything in
> heaven above or on the earth beneath or in the waters below. You
> shall not bow down to them or worship them; for I, the LORD your
> God, am a jealous God, punishing the children for the sin of the
> fathers to the third and fourth generation of those who hate me, but
> showing love to a thousand generations of those who love me and
> keep my commandments.
> You shall not misuse the name of the LORD your God, for the LORD will
> not hold anyone guiltless who misuses his name."

God doesn't call us to worship him because he has a weak ego that needs to be massaged. Instead, God calls us to worship him for our own good. It is in worshiping God that life begins to open up. As we worship God, the rest of life begins to fall into place. We begin to realize that at the heart of the cosmos is a God who loves us. We actually matter to him!

God created us to worship him alone because to lean the ladder of our lives against a different wall is to invite a great crash. God is the only being who is great enough and reliable enough to deserve our ultimate faith and trust in this life.

Question 26. Isn't God kind of old and boring?

James Joyce wrote a book titled *Portrait of the Artist as a Young Man*. The main character is a young man named Steven who is seriously considering devoting his life to Christ. But when Steven meets a priest, he notices that the priest's life is dull, boring and drab. In sharp contrast to a life devoted to God is the life devoted to art. The pursuit of art is a passionate pursuit, full of beauty and creativity. Steven obviously chooses not to devote his life to a dull, boring, drab God but instead to pursue art with all the passion and creativity he can muster.

Steven missed the goodness of God in all its beauty, passion and creativity. Steven settled for a caricature of God that was dull, boring and drab. But that is a false caricature. For the Bible reveals that God is the God who created art and our ability to experience passion, beauty and creativity. God, in his very character, is creatively and passionately good. That is why the psalmist wrote:

> Shout for joy to the LORD, all the earth.
>> Worship the LORD with gladness;
>> come before him with joyful songs.
> Know that the LORD is God.
>> It is he who made us, and we are his;
>> we are his people, the sheep of his pasture.
> Enter his gates with thanksgiving
>> and his courts with praise;
>> give thanks to him and praise his name.

For the LORD is good and his love endures forever;
his faithfulness continues through all generations. (Psalm 100)

Because God is good, the theme of joy fills the Bible. Nehemiah 8:10 says, "The joy of the LORD is your strength." The Old Testament prophet Habakkuk clearly outlined the violence and chaos of living in the real world, but at the conclusion of his book he wrote, "Though the fig tree does not bud / and there are no grapes on the vines, / though the olive crop fails / and the fields produce no food, / though there are no sheep in the pen / and no cattle in the stalls, / yet I will rejoice in the LORD, / I will be joyful in God my Savior" (Habakkuk 3:17-18). Jesus said to his disciples shortly before he was crucified, "As the Father has loved me, so have I loved you. Now remain in my love. If you obey my commands, you will remain in my love, just as I have obeyed my Father's commands and remain in his love. I have told you this so that my joy may be in you and that your joy may be complete" (John 15:9-11).

Drab human goodness says, "Do not throw wild parties." But Jesus said, "When you give a banquet, invite the poor, the crippled, the lame, the blind, and you will be blessed. Although they cannot repay you, you will be repaid at the resurrection of the righteous" (Luke 14:13-14). The point is simple. When you and I live in a spiritual relationship with the living God, his goodness and love produce joy in our lives. As we experience God's goodness, he produces in us a desire to be passionately and creatively good.

Question 27. How do I know I can trust God?

On September 18, 1982, the United States government released the results of a painful investigation. The government determined that a soldier stationed in South Korea had defected to the Communists. On August 28 of that year, a twenty-one-year-old private willingly walked across the Korean demilitarized zone into North Korea "for motives that are not known." He refused to come back in spite of the fact that his fellow American soldiers pleaded with him to return.

The day after the government released its report, the parents of the young man held a news conference on the lawn of their St. Louis home. With tears flowing freely down his cheeks, the father said that the family had accepted the fact that their son was indeed a defector. "He has lost his credibility in this country, even with me," said the man. But then he showed the heart of a father. "I still love my son," he said, "and want him back."

God is just like the father of that young soldier. You and I have turned our backs on him and walked away. But the light is on. The door is open. And the father is waiting for you and me to return home.

Throughout the Old Testament, one of the predominant themes is God's call on the Israelite people to separate themselves from the idols of the cultures surrounding them. He called them to worship him alone, the one true, living God. How ironic that after thousands of years, the human race still struggles with the same old problem of idolatry.

Idolatry can be the worship of a metal image or the worship of a mental picture. The narcissist worships self. The entrepreneur worships a career. The materialist worships money and the expensive toys money can buy. The athlete worships the perfect game or the perfect body. And Jesus weeps because people worship the gift instead of the author of the good gift. God hurts because people follow idols that lead only to destruction.

Against the background of human beings' changing caricatures of God, the Bible reveals that the true God is eternal and does not change in his character. God is no illusionist who alters himself according to people's whims. God is not an illusion who changes because of my creative fancy. God does not change because human beings have some new improved version of God.

Because God does not change, we never have to fear that he will be in a bad mood or have a bad day. We never have to worry that God will put a "do not disturb" sign on heaven's door. We never have to fear that God is having such an important discussion with someone else that he is too busy to listen to us.

The Bible gives many assurances such as these: "He who is the Glory of Israel does not lie or change his mind; for he is not a man, that he should change his mind" (1 Samuel 15:29). God revealed through the Hebrew prophet Malachi, "I the LORD do not change" (Malachi 3:6). Hebrews 13:8 tells us, "Jesus Christ is the same yesterday and today and forever." James wrote, "Every good and perfect gift is from above, coming down from the Father of the heavenly lights who does not change like shifting shadows" (James 1:17).

Jesus revealed that the Father even has the hairs of our head numbered (Matthew 10:30)! Therefore, we do not need to be afraid. The fact that God is eternal and does not change produces security and spiritual intimacy in our relationship with him. That is the good news.

The difficult news is that because God does not change, in order for God and us to get along, we are the ones who have to change. Jesus stated, "I tell you the truth, unless you change and become like little children, you will never enter the kingdom of heaven" (Matthew 18:3). Jesus repeatedly called people to repent of wrong attitudes and actions.

To repent means to radically change. To repent means to turn away from believing in illusions to believing in the true, eternal God. To repent means to no longer use God's legitimate gifts in illegitimate ways. To repent means to stop living in sexual immorality and to start living a sexually pure life. To repent means to no longer be motivated by greed but rather to be motivated by gratefulness to God. To repent means to turn away from hatred and revenge and to turn to loving and forgiving people. To repent means to turn away from laziness and to begin to work hard motivated by a desire to serve God as we serve people. To repent means to turn away from dehumanizing people through racist and sexist attitudes and to start respecting and encouraging all people as human beings created in the image of God.

When we do that, we find that our heavenly Father, like the father of the soldier who defected to North Korea, still loves us and welcomes us back. We find we can really trust him after all.

Question 28. Can't I worship God without worshiping Jesus?

Jesus made many bold and even shocking statements about himself. One of them was "I am the light of the world. Whoever follows me will never walk in darkness, but will have the light of life" (John 8:12). To be lost in darkness is a horrible waste of time and life. Jesus claims to be God in the flesh, offering us purpose, meaning and direction for our lives.

Jesus calls us to follow him completely. He asks for the kind of total allegiance which only God deserves. Why should we pay any attention to those outrageous claims? Why should we worship and follow Jesus?

I would like to suggest nine reasons you and I should worship and follow Jesus. There are of course many others!

First, you and I need a spiritual birth and growth. Because you and I have rebelled against God, we are spiritually dead. When we put our faith in Christ, he makes us spiritually alive. To follow Jesus means that we will spiritually grow. God created us to know and enjoy him forever. True spirituality is not something we make up as we go through life. True spirituality is being connected to the living God. True spirituality develops as we follow Jesus Christ closely. As we follow Christ, we get to know God better and to enjoy him more profoundly.

Second, when we follow Jesus Christ, our marriages become the joyful, fulfilling relationships that God intended them to be. When we seriously put our faith in Jesus, our marriages are not simply a personal commitment made between two people. When we follow Jesus, our marriages become an outgrowth to him. It is within the context of this profound spiritual commitment that we are free to sacrificially love each other, to give each other room to grow and to forgive each other.

Third, to follow Jesus means that we have a new attitude toward our work. No longer is financial reward the primary motivation to work. To follow Jesus means to realize that we are created in the image of a God who delights in creatively working. God has given us the abilities and talents to provide a good service and to produce a good product in order to make this world a better place to live. God has wired us in such a way that we can experience an appropriate rush of adrenaline when we do a good job. There is a sense of accomplishment and satisfaction. This appreciation of work is the opposite of laziness. To follow Jesus means that the primary motive for our work is to serve God and people by using the talents God has given us in a responsible way. We work to make this world more like heaven will be.

Fourth, to follow Jesus means that we are free from pride and free to be humble in a reasonable manner. When we begin to realize that only God is great, we are free to acknowledge that we are his creatures, his children. This frees us from having to posture ourselves as superior to others. This allows us to treat all people with equal respect, including ourselves. To follow Jesus means that our significance comes from him. Instead of turning to prosperity, popularity, power or position as the basis of our significance, we realize that he made us and that he loves us. It is because God made us for a purpose and loves us unconditionally that we have true significance.

Fifth, to follow Jesus means to understand that God created us with a healthy ambition. Instead of focusing our ambition on self-promotion, we will focus our ambition on building the kingdom of Christ and living for his glory. This means we will work against human suffering and spiritual blindness. We will work to promote life and spiritual vitality.

Sixth, to follow Jesus means to enjoy the bodies God has given us. Physical pleasure is a gift from God. But physical pleasure must never become the goal of our lives. Physical pleasure must always be enjoyed within the context of God's will, for only God is wise enough to set the context in which physical pleasure will be enjoyed and will not be allowed to enslave and dehumanize us.

Seventh, to follow Jesus means that we will become passionate people. It seems that in America we are only passionate about sex. But God is passionate about you and me. He really cares about us. We really matter to him. To follow Jesus means that we become passionate about God and each other. We care deeply about God and about each other.

Eighth, to follow Jesus means that we grow in wisdom. Wisdom is the ability to apply God's truth to everyday life. Wisdom flows from having God's perspective on life. It is not enough to simply be smart. We need to be able to make decisions that will benefit others and ourselves in this life. Life gets too complex for us human beings, left to our own devices, to make the wisest decisions. We need God's perspective. We need to understand what his will is in a given situation. God grants wisdom to those who ask him.

Ninth, to follow Jesus means that he will go with us through death out the other side to eternal life. A friend said to me, paraphrasing Psalm 23, "Even though I walk through the valley of the shadow of death, I will fear no evil. Because I am big." We both got a good laugh at that. Yet unfortunately, that is the attitude of too many people. What a farce! Confronted by the ultimate human dilemma—death—we need God.

Jesus is God come to the rescue. Jesus promises eternal life in heaven to all who follow him. It takes the supernatural God to beat death. Jesus is the supernatural God revealing himself in a form that you and I can understand. Jesus clearly says to you and to me, "Follow me!" The reality of the complexity of life and the finality of death highlights the fact that it is most reasonable to follow Jesus Christ.

Bertrand Russell, the famous atheistic philosopher, is supposed to have written once, "The center of me is always and eternally a terrible pain—a curious, wild pain—a searching for something beyond what the world contains, something transfigured and infinite, the beatific vision—God. I do not find it, I do not think it is to be found, but the love of it is my life; it's like passionate love for a ghost. At times it fills me with rage, at times with wild despair; it is the source of gentleness and cruelty and work; it fills every passion I have. It is the actual spring of life in me."

I love it! Russell acknowledged that this world was not capable of meeting some of his deepest longings. He was searching for God. Why did he conclude that God was not to be found? Jesus Christ is God revealing himself in a way that you and I—even with our finite, limited minds—can understand.

A young man said to me, "Cliffe, growing up I went to church on Christmas and Easter. Christianity was a dead religion for me. It wasn't until I began to understand that Jesus Christ died on the cross for me that something began to change within me. I realized that Jesus did not have to die for me. I began to realize that Jesus did not have to go through the horrible death of crucifixion. He could have died some other way. But he went through the horror of the cross to forgive me of my sin and to give me eternal life. Cliffe, when I began to understand that, something began to change inside me. Jesus Christ became very real and very personal to me. I stand in wonder of him."

Christianity is an historical religion. All religions obviously have historical events. But faith in Christ is not faith in a series of teachings given by an instructor. Rather faith in Christ is faith in a personal being, the Lord Jesus Christ, the living God. If you take Buddha out of Buddhism, you still have a wonderful body of teachings and a religion that is intact. If you take Muhammad out of Islam, you still have a wonderful body of teachings in the Koran that comprises a highly respected religion. But if you take Jesus Christ out of Christianity, the whole thing falls apart.

When you and I are confronted by Jesus, the main issue is not "Do you agree with his teachings?" Rather the issue is "Is Jesus the truth?"

Since God has given more than enough evidence for any thinking person to believe in him, what are some of the reasons that people reject God? I am afraid that the following dialogue is too frequently the real reason people reject Christ.

While speaking on Red Square at the University of Washington, I recognized a young man in the audience. I asked, "Greg Lewis, is that you?" He nodded. I said, "Greg, please come down and explain to the students how you have come to your faith in Christ." Greg Lewis had become the leading rusher on the University of Washington football team. During the last game of the season, he injured his knee and was told by the doctors that he needed an operation. He refused to have the operation and played in the Rose Bowl, where he was the leading rusher. Greg said, "Knees do not heal themselves of the type of injury I had. Jesus Christ healed me." I thanked Greg as he made his way back into the crowd.

Suddenly a young man announced, "I pity you both. You have both given up your wills in order to obey Jesus Christ. You are pathetic human beings. I'm not sure I still would call you really human. I would rather go to hell with my will intact than to go to heaven by giving up my will to God. I will never allow Jesus Christ to tell me what to do."

After a few seconds of being in silent shock, I responded, "When Greg and I say that we trust Christ and submit to his will, it does not mean that we become less human. Rather, it does mean that we are trusting the God who created us as humans to define what real humanness is to look like. When Greg and I trusted Christ and chose to follow him, the only freedom we gave up was the freedom to hurt others and to hurt ourselves. Because Jesus loves us, he tells us how we can enjoy life in all its breadth and beauty. Part of what it means to trust in Jesus Christ is that I want to become like the best person who ever walked the planet, Jesus Christ. Greg and I are not God's robots. We are Christ's men who are enjoying the freedom of living life as God intended us to live it. That is real freedom. That is what it means to be a real human being."

Only God, revealed in Jesus Christ, is worthy of our worship. Jesus promises us eternal life with him in heaven. When we choose to put our faith in him and to worship him daily by living our lives for him, we can be sure we will spend eternity together with him and worshiping him in heaven.

We all struggle with doubt.
The question is,
What will you and I do
with our doubts?
Will we allow our doubts
to drive us into skepticism
and cynicism?
Or will we allow our doubts
to motivate us
to study the evidence
more carefully?

8

Can you help me believe?

Advertising put the Nike shoe company on the map. Phil Knight founded Nike in 1972, and after two decades it was one of the best known companies in the world. When you think of Nike, you think of the phrase "Just do it." Or you think of Spike Lee muttering about Michael Jordan, "It's gotta be the shoes." Or Charles Barclay announcing, "Just because I can dunk a basketball doesn't mean I should raise your kids."

Nike was named advertiser of the year in 1994 at the Cannes International Advertising Festival. This is incredible in light of Phil Knight's horrible view of advertising at one point. In fact in 1981, when Phil Knight hired a new ad agency, he met with the agency's president and said, "I hate advertising!"

The greatest advertiser in the world once hated advertising! And all of us, at some point, have hated or resented God. But God can change our attitudes. He does it by changing us on the inside.

Maybe you think you're beyond hope, you could never find faith, you could never be a Christian. If you trust Jesus, he will enter your life and transform you from the inside out and make you into into a real believer.

Question 29. What does it mean to accept Jesus as Savior?

To accept Jesus means to put your trust, faith, loyalty and confidence in Christ. It means to trust that he died on the cross to forgive your sin and to give you the gift of eternal life.

To accept Jesus means to trust him totally. It means that with your mind you acknowledge that he is trustworthy. It means that with your will you submit to his will. It means that with your emotions you respond to his love by loving him.

The Bible talks a lot about having a heart for God. When the Bible uses the word *heart,* it is referring to this combination of mind, will and emotions. When you accept Jesus, you commit your life to him with your mind, your will and your emotions. You give your heart to Jesus.

A fire broke out in a psychiatric hospital. The fire fighters rushed to the hospital and began to rescue the patients. Suddenly they heard voices crying out for help from the rear of the hospital. Some fire fighters ran around to the back of the building and saw three men standing on a third floor balcony calling for help.

Quickly they opened up a net and called for the trapped men to jump into it. Two of the three jumped from the third floor balcony into the net. The third man refused to jump. He refused to trust the net. He refused to believe the net could catch him. Instead, he turned and walked into the burning psychiatric hospital.

After the fire had been put out, the fire fighters found the burned, charred body of that one patient. Because the man refused to believe in the fire fighters and in the net they held open for him, he perished in the fire.

Jesus continues to warn us that if we do not believe in him, we will perish. He promises that if we do believe in him, he will give us life with God now and eternal life in heaven.

To believe in Jesus is crucial. It is our belief in Jesus that God honors by forgiving us and giving us eternal life. It is our refusal to believe in Jesus that God holds us accountable for. If we refuse to believe in Jesus, we are responsible to pay the penalty for our own sin. If we refuse to believe in Jesus, we are deciding to live our lives separate from God. That decision has eternal consequences. We will spend eternity separate from God. But if we believe in Jesus, we are making a decision to live life together with God. That decision will also have eternal consequences. We will spend eternity together with Jesus in heaven.

Question 30. As long as I believe in Christ in my heart, why is it anybody else's business how I live?

A student asked me, "When I accept Jesus and trust him to give me eternal life, can I live any way I want?" My response was simple: "Jesus has an embarrassing way of combining spirituality with ethics. In America, spirituality divorced from ethics is very popular. It's popular to be spiritual and then to go out and live any way I want to live. But Jesus had an uncanny way of linking my spirituality with my ethics."

For example, Jesus had an embarrassing way of linking my faith in him with how I should love all people. When he was asked which of God's commandments is most important, he responded, "The most important one . . . is this: 'Hear, O Israel, the Lord our God, the Lord is one. Love the Lord your God with all your heart and with all your soul and with all your mind and with all your strength.' The second is this: 'Love your neighbor as yourself.' There is no commandment greater than these" (Mark 12:29-31).

The apostle John wrote, "If anyone says, 'I love God,' yet hates his brother, he is a liar. For anyone who does not love his brother, whom he has seen, cannot love God, whom he has not seen. And he has given us this command: Whoever loves God must also love his brother" (1 John 4:20-21). If I hate other people, it shows that I do not genuinely trust in Christ.

Do followers of Christ struggle with hatred? Absolutely yes. But the point is, genuine followers of Christ struggle against hatred. Their faith is in Christ. Their genuine desire is to obey him in their ethics. A genuine follower of Christ asks Christ for the help to love all people.

Jesus strongly disagrees with current American culture, which tells us that one's spirituality is a private matter which doesn't need to have any impact on one's lifestyle. When you and I put our faith in Christ, he comes in as the manager, the CEO, the boss of every area of our lives.

Jesus wants to readjust our priorities. Jesus wants to fill us with his Holy Spirit to control our tongues. Jesus calls us to live sexually pure lives. He calls us to be content and not to covet. He calls us to work hard and earn money and share with those who are less fortunate. He calls us to use our power in a way that builds people up, not tears them down. He calls us to enjoy competition but not to seek to destroy people in our competitive urges. Jesus calls us not to seek revenge but to forgive. If a person puts faith in Christ, that person's spiritual relationship with Jesus will have a major impact on every area of life.

What does it mean to believe? It means to rely upon Jesus. It means to believe that Jesus bled and died on the cross for my sin. It means that I rely upon Jesus' death on the cross as the vehicle through which God forgives me and gives me eternal life. Jesus promises eternal life to all who rely, or believe, in him.

Question 31. Isn't fear of death a poor motive for believing in Jesus?

At Columbia University in New York City, a student stepped out of the crowd and said, "Cliffe, it seems to me the primary motive to believe in Jesus is fear of death. I have come to terms with my death. How would you try to motivate me to believe in Jesus?"

My first response is that my first motive in trusting Christ is not the fear of death. It is the affirmation of life. Jesus said, "The thief comes only to steal and kill and destroy; I have come that they may have life and have it to the full" (John 10:10). He also said, "I am the resurrection and the life. He who believes in me will live, even though he dies" (John 11:25).

I affirm the value of my life. I affirm the excitement I have in living!

Jesus Christ promises joy to those who surrender their lives to him. Jesus Christ promises eternal life to all who trust in him. The primary reason that I do not go out and play in traffic is because I affirm the value of my life. The primary reason that I believe in Jesus Christ is because of the way he affirms the value of my life.

What do we mean when we say, "I have come to terms with my own death"? I appreciate the honesty of Woody Allen when he said, "I am not afraid to die. I just don't want to be there when it happens." I appreciate his frankness when he said, "Who cares about achieving immortality through one's achievements? I'm interested in achieving immortality through not dying," and "Who cares about living on in the minds of my fans? I'm interested in living on in my apartment."

When you get sick, you go to a highly trained doctor to get well. You would rather live than die. Let's not lie to ourselves. The thought of our own death is not a pleasant one. But Christianity offers us hope for life beyond death, because Jesus has conquered death.

The most startling and earth-shaking event in human history has to do with life and death. The Gospel of John (20:1-9) gives the following account of what happened on the Sunday morning after Jesus was crucified:

> Early on the first day of the week, while it was still dark, Mary Magdalene went to the tomb and saw that the stone had been removed from the entrance. So she came running to Simon Peter and the other disciple, the one Jesus loved, and said, "They have taken the Lord out of the tomb, and we don't know where they have put him!"
>
> So Peter and the other disciple started for the tomb. Both were running, but the other disciple outran Peter and reached the tomb first. He bent over and looked in at the strips of linen lying there but did not go in. Then Simon Peter, who was behind him, arrived and went into the tomb. He saw the strips of linen lying there, as well as the burial cloth that had been around Jesus' head. The cloth was folded up by itself, separate from the linen. Finally, the other disciple, who had reached the tomb first, also went inside. He saw and believed. (They still did not understand from Scripture that Jesus had to rise from the dead.)

The historical resurrection of Jesus Christ is the foundation for belief that there is life after death. Obviously Jesus did not rise from the dead if there is no supernatural God. If there is no supernatural God, you and I live in a closed universe made up of matter and energy. But the evidence of the order and design of the cosmos points to the existence of some type of supernatural creator. The existence of moral absolutes points to some type of God existing before human beings who created and defined those moral absolutes.

Once you allow for the existence of a supernatural God, it is most reasonable to believe that this supernatural God could raise the dead. John ("the other disciple") recorded that when he saw the empty tomb and the empty grave clothes, he believed in Jesus. That's how the good news of Jesus' resurrection should affect us too—to trust in Jesus and accept him as Savior.

The evening after Peter and John ran to the empty tomb, Jesus showed himself alive to more of the disciples.

> On the evening of that first day of the week, when the disciples were together, with the doors locked for fear of the Jews, Jesus came and stood among them and said, "Peace be with you!" After he said this, he showed them his hands and side. The disciples were overjoyed when they saw the Lord.
>
> Again Jesus said, "Peace be with you! As the Father has sent me, I am sending you." And with that he breathed on them and said, "Receive the Holy Spirit." (John 20:19-22)

It is interesting that Jesus repeated to his fearful disciples, "Peace be with you." The disciples thought all their hopes were dead. They knew very well that Jesus had died on a Roman cross. The fact that they had locked the doors shows us they were afraid for their own lives. Faced with the reality of death, whether our own or someone else's, we are in desperate need of Christ's peace. Ernest Becker concluded that "what has been taking place on the planet for about three billion years is that it is being turned into a vast pit of fertilizer." No wonder so many Americans consume huge quantities of tranquilizers, alcohol, sleeping pills and other drugs in the quest for some type of tranquillity.

To people crushed by the uncertainty and finality of death, Jesus says, "Peace be with you." But this peace is reserved only for those who trust in Christ and commit their lives to him. When Peter and John saw the empty tomb, they believed in Jesus. When the disciples saw Jesus risen from the dead, they moved from fear to faith, from skepticism to belief. That is the exact change that Jesus calls you and me to make.

Question 32. Is it a sin to have doubts?

We tend to look down on someone who is called a "doubting Thomas." We imagine that Thomas lacked a strong faith. The Bible is much kinder to the doubting apostle than we might expect. Here's the story of how he got his unfortunate reputation:

> Now Thomas (called Didymus), one of the twelve, was not with the disciples when Jesus came. So the other disciples told him, "We have seen the Lord!"
>
> But he said to them, "Unless I see the nail marks in his hands and put my finger where the nails were, and put my hand into his side, I will not believe it."
>
> A week later, his disciples were in the house again, and Thomas was with them. Though the doors were locked, Jesus came and stood among them and said, "Peace be with you!" Then he said to Thomas, "Put your finger here; see my hands. Reach out your hand and put it into my side. Stop doubting and believe."
>
> Thomas said to him, "My Lord and my God!"
>
> Then Jesus told him, "Because you have seen me, you have believed; blessed are those who have not seen and yet have believed." (John 20:24-29)

Thomas was not playing mind games with Jesus. Once when Jesus told his disciples that he was headed back to a place where people had tried to stone him, Thomas said to the rest of them, "Let us also go, that we may die with him" (John 11:16). Thomas did not have a history of being wishy-washy in his commitment to Christ.

At this point Thomas was honestly struggling to know whether Jesus was the Christ or not. Jesus' death had been a shattering experience for Thomas and for all the disciples. When the other disciples insisted they had seen Jesus risen from the dead, it was too much for Thomas to believe. Rising from the dead isn't something that happens every day! But when Jesus appeared to Thomas alive, his doubts vanished, and he embraced Jesus.

We all struggle with doubt. The question is, What will you and I do with our doubts? Will we allow our doubts to drive us into skepticism and cynicism? Or will we allow our doubts to motivate us to study the evidence more carefully?

There are too many people today who worship the search. There are too many people today who enjoy agnosticism. There are too many people today who insist, "I cannot know whether Jesus is reliable or not." But agnosticism, living in "no-man's-land," is not a practical option.

If Romeo says to Juliet, "I love you. Will you marry me?" and Juliet responds, "I don't know. We'll have to wait till tomorrow," Juliet is making a decision. The decision is to not marry Romeo at this point. If the next day Romeo expresses his love and his desire to marry her, and once again Juliet responds, "I don't know. We'll just have to wait and see," Juliet is making a further decision. If this pattern continues, then Romeo and Juliet will die unmarried—at least to each other.

Love does not force. Love waits patiently for a response. But if the response is, "I do not know. I do not know. I do not know. I do not know," then that is a decision. The decision is to not respond positively to the person who is communicating love to you.

Jesus loved Thomas. Confronted by the evidence of Jesus' reliability, Thomas responded to Jesus' love in faith. Jesus loves you. How will you respond to his love?

Question 33. How can anyone interpret the Bible accurately?

Another Columbia University student asked, "How do you interpret the Bible? The fundamentalists have one interpretation. The liberals have another. The Republicans have another. The Democrats have another. How can you expect me to interpret the Bible accurately?"

I responded, "Interpret the Bible the same way you would interpret any text here at Columbia University. Respect literary style. If it's poetry, read it as poetry. If it's a science textbook, read it as a science textbook. If it's historical narrative, read it as historical narrative. And always read in context. Never take one line out of a text and conclude that is the worldview of the author."

The Bible includes various literary styles. You will find poetry, moral teaching, historical narrative, parable and apocalyptic literature in the Bible. Respect the different literary styles. When Jesus says, "I am the light of the world," it is irresponsible to interpret that to mean that Jesus is claiming to be a thousand-watt light bulb. You must allow a speaker or author to use simile, metaphor or allegory.

Read in context. Do not rip one line out of the text and insist that that is the main point of the author or speaker. Read the gospels through in their entirety. Interpret the teachings of Christ within the context of all of his teachings found in the gospels.

In interpreting the Bible, it is very important that we allow ourselves to be guided by God's Holy Spirit. If you are genuine in wanting to know God, he will help you by his Holy Spirit. The apostle Paul wrote that "the man without the Spirit does not accept the things that come from the Spirit of God, for they are foolishness to him, and he cannot understand them, because they are spiritually discerned" (1 Corinthians 2:14). Be open to God's Spirit. Allow the Holy Spirit to guide you as you read the Bible.

Question 34. Aren't there a lot of unanswered questions in the Bible?

At the end of his Gospel the apostle John wrote, "Jesus did many other miraculous signs in the presence of his disciples, which are not recorded in this book. But these are written that you may believe that Jesus is the Christ, the Son of God, and that by believing you may have life in his name" (John 20:30-31).

John tells us why he wrote what he wrote, but he sure leaves us wondering about all the other things he could have written!

Aren't there many unanswered questions in the Bible? Absolutely yes. The Bible is about 1,600 pages long. It begins with the creation of the world. It ends with the return of Jesus Christ. That is an awful lot of years to cover in 1,600 pages. Obviously there are going to be many gaps. Obviously there are going to be many unanswered questions.

The Gospels of Matthew, Mark, Luke and John are historically reliable. The evidence of their internal consistency, the literary style of historical narrative they all employ, the fact that archaeology supports the place names and the over five thousand Greek manuscripts that they are based on all point to the historicity of the Gospels.

John was telling his readers, including you and me, that he wrote the Gospel of John for a purpose. That purpose is crystal clear. John was not trying to explain everything or give every detail. He wrote so that you and I may believe that Jesus is the Christ, the Son of God, and that by believing in Jesus you and I might have life.

To believe in Jesus is to become transformed inwardly and become spiritually alive to God. Paul wrote, "Do not conform any longer to the pattern of this world, but be transformed by the renewing of your mind" (Romans 12:2). The Greek word for "transformed" is the root of our word *metamorphosis*. Metamorphosis is a change from one form to another. It's the tadpole turning into a frog. It's the caterpillar turning into a butterfly. Paul also wrote, "And we, who with unveiled faces all reflect the Lord's glory, are being transformed into his likeness with ever-increasing glory, which comes from the Lord, who is the Spirit" (2 Corinthians 3:18).

When you and I put our faith in Jesus Christ, he puts his Holy Spirit in us. As you and I yield to the Holy Spirit, he changes us to be more and more like Christ.

Do you believe in Jesus? If you don't yet, I pray you will make that decision right now. Simply but profoundly, ask Jesus to forgive you for your wrongdoing. Simply but profoundly, trust that Jesus died on the cross to forgive you and give you eternal life. Simply but profoundly, ask Jesus to put his Holy Spirit in you. Trust him with your mind. Submit to his will. Love him with your emotions. When you make that decision to believe in Jesus, he promises to give you life with God now and for eternity.

Moses was crippled
by impulsive anger.
God had a mission for him.
Samson slept
with a Philistine whore.
But God had a mission for him. . . .
Peter was a cussing,
Christ-denying failure.
But Christ had a mission for him.

9

Can you help my faith grow?

Nobody wants to make a big commitment to a small God. It takes a big God for me to make a big commitment. Harold Kushner writes in *Who Needs God:*

> The next time you go to the zoo, notice where the lines are longest and people take the most time in front of the cage. We tend to walk briskly past the deer and the antelope with only a passing glance at their graceful beauty. If we have children, we may pause to enjoy the antics of the seals and the monkeys, but we find ourselves irresistibly drawn to the lions, the tigers, the elephants, the gorillas. Why? I suspect that without realizing or understanding it, we are strangely reassured by seeing creatures bigger or stronger than ourselves. It gives us the message, at once humbling and comforting, that we are not the ultimate power. Our souls are so starved for that sense of awe, that encounter with grandeur which helps to remind us of our real place in the universe, that if we can't get it in church, we will search for it and find it someplace else.

God created us with a need to stand in awe of him. A growing faith is based on a growing vision of Christ's greatness. A big commitment to Christ requires a big vision of Christ. As we grow in our understanding of God's greatness, his power and his love for us, we grow in our commitment to him.

The great Russian novelist Feodor Dostoyevsky wrote, "The one essential condition of human existence is that man should always be able to bow down to something infinitely great. The infinite and the eternal are as essential for man as the little planet on which he dwells." It is essential in order for you and me to become truly human to grasp that God is infinite and eternal. When we grasp this reality, our faith deepens and our commitment grows. We begin to realize how ludicrous it is to say, "Everything is yours, Lord, except this relationship, this deal, this pleasure." That line of thinking is beyond spiritual logic. When we realize the bigness of God, it is absurd to hold back any area of our lives from his control.

Sam Shoemaker once wrote, "To be a Christian means to give as much of myself as I can to as much of Jesus as I know." When our lives are governed on a daily basis by that attitude, our faith cannot help but grow.

Question 35. Does faith grow naturally, or are there things I can do to help it along?

My faith grows as I obey Jesus. As I put into practice what Jesus says, I see that his teachings work. They make sense. Observing this fact causes my faith in Jesus to deepen.

Faith in Christ also grows as we serve each other. Get involved in people's lives by serving them Jesus style. As you minister in Christ's name, your faith will grow. Paul encouraged us, "Be devoted to one another in brotherly love. Honor one another above yourselves" (Romans 12:10).

Devotion is an uncommon quality today, but Jesus commands it. Jesus is a friend who walks in when the world has walked out. In Jesus' day the world walked out on lepers, tax collectors, zealots, prostitutes, the wealthy and the poor. Jesus walked into those people's lives as their best friend.

Jesus realizes that even if you have made a wreck of your life, you have not done a permanent job. Jesus knows the great things he can do through each one of us once we surrender our lives to him. He does not wash his hands of failures the way Pontius Pilate did. The Bible says, "God demonstrates his own love for us in this: While we were still sinners, Christ died for us" (Romans 5:8). That is the type of devotion Christ calls you and me to have for one another.

In his book *The Coach's Son* Gene Stallings talks about his special relationship with his son Johnny. While Gene was an assistant football coach to the legendary Bear Bryant, he and his wife Ruthie had a baby boy. Immediately following the birth, the doctor conferred with Gene in the hallway. He said, "We think maybe your baby has Down Syndrome." Returning to his wife, Gene said, "Ruthie, the doctor just gave me some bad news. I'm not sure if he really knows, but he said there's something the matter with our little boy—that maybe he is retarded."

"That can't be true! The doctor is mistaken. He can't be certain!" Ruthie said again and again. Gene felt helpless as he stood at the end of her bed and watched her cry. Further tests confirmed that indeed little Johnny had Down syndrome.

Friends encouraged Gene and Ruthie to institutionalize their son. He would be an embarrassment, a burden, a hindrance to Gene's career and a drain on Ruth. Eventually Gene and Ruth would have to live their lives as if Johnny did not exist. But Gene and Ruthie concluded, "The fact was, Johnny was ours to love."

Gene would sit next to Johnny's crib watching him sleep. "I was falling in love with my son," he admitted. Because Johnny had a difficult time breathing, doctors said that he could not take anesthesia. Gene wondered how he and Ruthie could live with the constant fear of an injury possibly ending Johnny's life.

Gene left the University of Alabama to go to Texas A & M as head football coach. His daughters began to teach Johnny to walk. One day, while Johnny sat in his lap in church, Gene felt some warm fluid seeping into his lap. He was shocked by the sight of blood flowing from Johnny's backside. They rushed Johnny to the hospital, where doctors said they would have to operate immediately because there was some sharp object slicing Johnny's intestines. Gene said, "He can't tolerate it. He's not supposed to have surgery because he cannot endure anesthesia." The doctors were insistent. They had to operate.

Gene ran down the hall and burst into the office of the anesthesiologist and shouted, "I want you to handle this exactly right. You give him enough, not a drop too much." The anesthesiologist responded, "Coach, I know you do the best job you can and I respect that, and you've got to trust me to do my job to the best of my ability." The surgery was a success. Johnny handled the anesthesia like a pro.

The night after the operation, Gene and Ruthie slept in cots in Johnny's room. Periodically, Gene would open his eyes during the night to look at his son lying in bed. Every time he did so, he saw the anesthesiologist sitting in a chair beside the bed stroking his little son Johnny. Johnny recovered fully from the surgery. Gene was fired from his position as head coach of the Texas A & M football team and later hired to be an assistant to Tom Landry of the Dallas Cowboys. Then the St. Louis Cardinals hired him as head coach, and he went with the Cardinals when they moved to Phoenix. After two losing seasons in Phoenix, Gene was fired. The University of Alabama called him and invited him to be head coach of their football team. In 1993, Gene Stallings led the University of Alabama football team to a national championship.

In 1996 Gene retired as football coach at the University of Alabama. At a press conference, Gene looked over and saw Johnny sitting next to his sisters sobbing. The next day he opened up the newspaper, and there on the back page of the sports section was a prominent color photograph of Johnny crying as his dad announced his resignation. When he saw that picture, Gene once again thanked God for the gift of his son. Johnny had taught his father so much about courage, about empathy and about being a father. "Good job, son," Gene whispered.

The heart is happiest when it beats for others. When you and I sacrificially give of ourselves to others, it shows that we value them highly. A man wrapped up in himself makes a very small package. Jesus sacrificially gave his life on the cross for you and for me. When we put our faith in Jesus, we are responding to his sacrificial love. Our response of faith shows that we begin to understand his sacrificial love. This understanding drives us to sacrificially give ourselves to others.

Question 36. What's the connection between prayer and faith?

Prayer is not an exercise in getting. Prayer is an experiment in intimacy. Paul told believers to be "faithful in prayer" (Romans 12:12). As we pray daily, our faith in Christ is strengthened. There are so many distractions in this world that can detach us from Jesus Christ. God has given us many good gifts to enjoy, but when we focus solely on the gifts, they detach us from the giver of those good gifts. There must be balance. As we daily pray, we focus our lives upon Jesus Christ. He is the one who sustains us.

Jesus' prayer life sustained him as he faced his last temptations in life. In the Garden of Gethsemane, he struggled with the prospect of going through the agony of the cross. He prayed, "Father, if you are willing, take this cup from me; yet not my will, but yours be done" (Luke 22:42). In prayer, Jesus surrendered to his Father's plan. Jesus struggled and decided to do it his Father's way. When Jesus was dying on the cross, his enemies taunted him. Instead of responding in vitriolic bitterness, he prayed, "Father, forgive them, for they do not know what they are doing" (Luke 23:34).

Jesus experienced the hiddenness of God. As he was hanging on the cross, his Father dumped the sins of the world on him. Jesus became sin for us. He was separated from the Father when he became sin. He cried out in his cosmic loneliness, "My God, my God, why have you forsaken me?" (Matthew 27:46). Jesus had spent eternity with his Father. Suddenly he was separated from him.

You and I also experience the hiddenness of God. In the midst of that cosmic loneliness, Jesus did not turn against his Father but chose to trust him. Never doubt in the dark what you know in the light. But that's not easy. That strength comes from being faithful in prayer. That strength comes from regularly being in communication with the living God. That strength comes from daily focusing on the Lord Jesus Christ.

On day six of the Apollo 13 mission, the astronauts needed to make a critical course correction by means of a thirty-nine-second burn of their main engines. If they failed, they would never make it home to planet Earth. In order to conserve power, they had shut down the computer that steered Apollo 13. The challenge now was how to steer the giant spacecraft.

Astronaut Jim Lovell decided that if he could find a fixed point in space, he would be able to manually steer the spacecraft toward it. The focal point he chose was their destination, planet Earth. For thirty-nine agonizing seconds Jim Lovell focused on planet Earth through a small window. By focusing intently upon their destination, the astronauts avoided disaster.

Daily prayer is a daily centering of ourselves in Christ. Faithfulness in prayer means to continually focus on the living God. The author of Hebrews wrote, "Let us fix our eyes on Jesus, the author and perfecter of our faith, who for the joy set before him endured the cross, scorning its shame, and sat down at the right hand of the throne of God. Consider him who endured such opposition from sinful men, so that you will not grow weary and lose heart" (12:2-3).

To talk to and to listen to God is a crucial way to build our faith. Detach yourself from all that distracts you from God. Attach yourself to Jesus in faithful prayer. Your faith will grow.

Question 37. I want a faith that's down-to-earth, for here and now. Is heaven really important?

Bill Russell said that after eleven championship seasons with the Boston Celtics, heaven was going to be a disappointment. The apostle Paul, however, had a different view of heaven when he wrote, "No eye has seen, no ear has heard, no mind has conceived what God has prepared for those who love him" (1 Corinthians 2:9). Because God is so good and so powerful and so creative, he has created delights in heaven that we cannot even begin to wrap our human minds around.

The skeptic Mark Twain commented that heaven will be boring because there will be no sex there. He forgot that the God who created the pleasure of sex is capable of creating something even better. I realize that this is difficult for the typical sex-crazed American to believe. All I can do is assure you that the God who created sex and gave it to us as a wonderful gift is more than capable of creating and giving to us even greater gifts.

"Be joyful in hope," the Bible says (Romans 12:12). Be joyful as you contemplate spending eternity with Jesus and loved ones in heaven! As the martyr Stephen was being stoned to death, he prayed, "Lord Jesus, receive my spirit" (Acts 7:59). Jesus told a thief who was dying beside him on a cross, "I tell you the truth, today you will be with me in paradise" (Luke 23:43). Paul wrote, "For to me, to live is Christ and to die is gain. If I am to go on living in the body, this will mean fruitful labor for me. Yet what shall I choose? I do not know! I am torn between the two: I desire to depart and to be with Christ, which is better by far" (Philippians 1:21-23). Paul also wrote, "Now we know that if the earthly tent we live in is destroyed, we have a building from God, an eternal house in heaven, not built by human hands" (2 Corinthians 5:1). Jesus assured us, "In my Father's house are many rooms; if it were not so, I would have told you. I am going there to prepare a place for you. And if I go and prepare a place for you, I will come back and take you to be with me that you also may be where I am" (John 14:2-3).

This hope of eternal life is not mere wishful thinking. It is a confident expectation of eternal life in heaven with Jesus and our loved ones based on the resurrection of Jesus Christ from the dead.

We look forward to the return of Jesus Christ when he will give us new bodies to live with him forever in heaven. Paul described this great coming event:

> For the Lord himself will come down from heaven, with a loud command, with the voice of the archangel and with the trumpet call of God, and the dead in Christ will rise first. After that, we who are still alive and are left will be caught up together with them in the clouds to meet the Lord in the air. And so we will be with the Lord forever. Therefore encourage one another with these words. (1 Thessalonians 4:16-18)

Insist upon a daily perspective that includes heaven. Allow the realization that Jesus loves you so much he wants to spend eternity with you in heaven to produce joy in your life.

Rick was a gold medal power lifter in the Olympics. In the spring of 1995, he spoke at a middle school assembly. After the program the principal asked him if he would visit a very special student. This student had an illness that kept him at home, but this student wanted desperately to meet Rick. Rick agreed to meet the young man. During the drive to the boy's home, Rick learned that Matthew had muscular dystrophy. When he was born, the doctors had told his parents that he would not live to see five. Then they told them that he would not live to see ten. He was now thirteen. He was a real fighter. Matthew wanted to meet Rick because Rick had overcome obstacles in achieving his dreams.

Rick and Matthew spoke for about an hour. Never once did Matthew complain and ask, "Why me?" He spoke about winning and succeeding and going for his dreams. He wasn't bitter over the cruel comments his classmates made. He focused instead on his hopes for the future. He wanted to lift weights with Rick.

When Rick and Matthew had finished talking, Rick went to his briefcase and pulled out the first gold medal he had won for power lifting and put it around Matthew's neck. Rick told Matthew he was more of a winner and knew more about overcoming obstacles than Rick ever would. Matthew looked at the medal for a while, took it off and handed it back to Rick. He said, "Rick, you are a champion. You earned that medal. Someday, when I get to the Olympics and win my gold medal, I will show it to you."

A while later, Rick received a letter from Matthew's parents informing him that Matthew had died. Matthew's parents wanted Rick to have a letter Matthew had written a few days before his death:

Dear Rick,

My mom said I should send you a thank you letter for the neat picture you sent me. I also wanted to let you know that the doctors tell me I don't have long to live anymore. It is getting very hard for me to breathe and I get tired very easy, but I still smile as much as I can. I know I will never be as strong as you, and I know that we will never get to lift weights together.

I told you someday I was going to go to the Olympics and win a gold medal. I know now I will never get to do that. But I know I am a champion, and God knows that too. He knows I am not a quitter and when I get to heaven, God will give me my gold medal, and when you get there, I will show it to you. Thanks for loving me.

Your friend, Matthew

We have a choice. We can either focus on death and despair, or we can focus on Jesus Christ, put our faith in him and celebrate the eternal life in heaven that he promises to all who follow him.

Question 38. I've accepted Christ, but I still have some of the same old problems—and even some new ones! Is there something wrong with my faith?

Paul tells us to be "patient in affliction" (Romans 12:12). This is one of the clearest ways to grow in your faith. To be patient in the midst of pain is to choose to acknowledge that God is good even when life is not. To be patient in the midst of affliction means to choose to trust Christ in the midst of pain instead of to choose to grow bitter against Christ.

In 1 Samuel 23—24 David (future king of Israel) is being hunted like a dog by King Saul. Consumed by jealousy, Saul wants to murder David. On two occasions, David is in a position to quickly terminate Saul's life. David could have chosen to listen to the voices in his head that said, *I want the throne now. I want instant gratification. Saul is an obstacle to my upward mobility. I will remove him now.* Instead, David chose to listen to the voice of the Spirit of God that said, "God has promised you the throne, David. Trust him to deliver on his schedule." As David exercised great patience in the midst of great affliction, David's faith and his relationship with God both grew.

James gives us some advice about being patient in affliction:

Be patient, then, brothers, until the Lord's coming. See how the farmer waits for the land to yield its valuable crop and how patient he is for the autumn and spring rains. You too, be patient and stand firm, because the Lord's coming is near. Don't grumble against each other, brothers, or you will be judged. The Judge is standing at the door!

Brothers, as an example of patience in the face of suffering, take the prophets who spoke in the name of the Lord. As you know, we consider blessed those who have persevered. You have heard of Job's perseverance and have seen what the Lord finally brought about. The Lord is full of compassion and mercy. (James 5:7-11)

Pain attacks our spiritual confidence. Pain often blocks us from constructive activity. Pain and death are often equated with failure and defeat. God seems to prefer a faith that seeks to change things rather than to give in to evil and resign oneself to evil. But God also seems to prefer a faith that chooses to trust him when it is impossible to change the circumstances. God seems to prefer a faith that acknowledges the unfairness of life but is willing to submit to God's timing instead of demanding our own timing.

God looks for a faith in you and in me that can live with mystery, with unanswered questions. Human arrogance demands an instant, total answer to all of its questions. Faith in Christ's character enables us to withstand unexplained pain. Job never understood why God allowed him to suffer so intensely. Job held on tightly to God's character still being good.

When you begin to understand that God is really good and that he calls us to live really good lives, that produces in you and in me a patience and perseverance in doing what is good even when it hurts.

Rosa Parks, mother of the civil rights movement, was arrested in 1955 for refusing to give up her bus seat to a white man. After many boycotts and protests, the United States Supreme Court ruled racial segregation unconstitutional. In *Quiet Strength* Parks writes,

> I have learned over the years that knowing what must be done does away with fear. When I sat down on the bus that day, I had no idea history was being made—I was only thinking of getting home. But I had made up my mind. After so many years of being a victim of the mistreatment my people suffered, not giving up my seat—and whatever I had to face afterwards—was not important. I did not feel any fear sitting there. I felt the Lord would give me the strength to endure whatever I had to

face. It was time for someone to stand up—or in my case, sit down. So I refused to move.

That is patience in affliction. Realize that God is good. Realize that Jesus is with you. Do what is good, even though it brings pain. Do not compromise with evil, even though you know it is the easier path to take. As you obey Jesus, your faith in him will grow.

Victor Frankl was humiliated, stripped of all his dignity, abused and tortured in a concentration camp of Adolf Hitler's. Although he was a highly educated man, Frankl was forced into slave labor. Many of his friends in the concentration camp died, not from the gas chambers, but because they were eaten up with rage against their oppressors. The humiliation and the overwhelming injustice was too much for them to take. They chose to die. Nobody killed them. They gave up on life.

Frankl was familiar with the teaching of Jesus in the Sermon on the Mount. He decided to do good to those who harmed him. He chose to love his enemies. When his captors asked him to scrub the toilets with a toothbrush, he did it twice. The first time was because they commanded him to. The second time was because he willed to. Frankl refused to be destroyed by his own hatred. He chose to love his enemies by turning an oppressive, humiliating situation into an opportunity to serve.

All of us are humiliated and hurt at times. We all must choose to view the negative situation either as an opportunity to become angry and hateful or as an opportunity to serve. That decision is crucial to whether or not we will grow in faith.

Question 39. Why is the Bible so important for growing in faith?

"Everything that was written in the past was written to teach us, so that through endurance and the encouragement of the Scriptures we might have hope" (Romans 15:4). Learning, memorizing and applying God's Word causes our faith to grow. When our consciences convict us of sin, God's Word assures us of his forgiveness and the fact that he does not put us on the back burner. He still has a mission for us in life.

People of the Bible show us that God keeps working with his people and therefore he will keep working with us. Abraham dabbled in self-serving lies. God still had a mission for him. Jacob was a cheater *par excellence*. God had a mission for him. Moses was crippled by impulsive anger. God had a mission for him. Samson slept with a Philistine whore. But God had a mission for him. Solomon had seven hundred wives and three hundred concubines. But God still had a mission for him. Peter was a cussing, Christ-denying failure. But Christ had a mission for him.

In Psalm 1:1-2 the psalmist calls us to detach from all that distracts us and focus on God's Word so we can build a more intimate spiritual relationship with the living God. "Blessed is the man who does not walk in the counsel of the wicked or stand in the way of sinners or sit in the seat of mockers. But his delight is in the law of the Lord, and on his law he meditates day and night." The psalmist tells us to wrap our hearts and minds around God's revelation of himself in his Word. It is as we meditate, reflect and focus on the living God that we develop spiritual stability and depth of character and experience God's blessing.

When you're being pulled into a cesspool of self-pity, allow God to speak to you through his Word, for example, with words such as these: "Rejoice in the Lord always. I will say it again: Rejoice! Let your gentleness be evident to all. The Lord is near. Do not be anxious about anything, but in everything, by prayer and petition, with thanksgiving, present your requests to God. And the peace of God, which transcends all understanding, will guard your hearts and your minds in Christ Jesus" (Philippians 4:4-7). Read these further words of Paul from prison: "I have learned to be content whatever the circumstances. I know what it is to be in need, and I know what it is to have plenty. I have learned the secret of being content in any and every situation, whether well fed or hungry, whether living in plenty or in want. I can do everything through Christ who gives me strength" (Philippians 4:11-13).

When you lose a loved one or when the doctor has bad news for you, let God speak to you through his Word with assurances such as this one:

Listen, I tell you a mystery: We will not all sleep, but we will all be changed—in a flash, in the twinkling of an eye, at the last trumpet. For the trumpet will sound, the dead will be raised imperishable, and we will be changed. For the perishable must clothe itself with the imperishable, and the mortal with immortality. When the perishable has been clothed with the imperishable, and the mortal with immortality, then the saying that is written will come true: "Death has been swallowed up in victory." (1 Corinthians 15:51-54)

When the sting of failure is very painful, let God speak to you through his Word. When the aging process begins to take its toll and what used to work no longer works, let God speak to you through his Word. Paul wrote these encouraging words: "Therefore, we do not lose heart. Though outwardly we are wasting away, yet inwardly we are being renewed day by day. For our light and momentary troubles are achieving for us an eternal glory that far outweighs them all. So we fix our eyes not on what is seen, but on what is unseen. For what is seen is temporary, but what is unseen is eternal" (2 Corinthians 4:16-18).

When the absurdity of life is crushing, and the mystery of life is perplexing, let God speak to you through his Word. Say what the young boy Samuel said: "Speak, Lord, for your servant is listening" (1 Samuel 3:9). Ma Bell does not have heaven's phone number listed. I have never received priority mail from heaven. But God has given us his Word.

As we reflect on God's Word, he will speak to us. As we pray and are silent before him, he will guide us. As we refuse to doubt in the dark what we know in the light, Jesus will lead us. As we trust an unknown future to a known God, he will guide us. Our faith will grow. We will stand firm. What a challenge! What a life!

CPSIA information can be obtained at www.ICGtesting.com
Printed in the USA
LVOW07s0208120216

474818LV00001B/54/P